This book is dedicated to the loyal readers of
The Georgia Mountain Laurel Magazine and
those who enjoy Rabun's Recipes. . .

Thank you!

P.O. Box 2218 • Clayton, Georgia
706-782-1608 • www.laurelpress.com

ISBN 978-0-9799834-0-5

Printed in the United States of America

Dear Readers,

I was both honored and humbled when my publisher Tracy McCoy called and said that she and the staff of The Georgia Mountain Laurel would like to publish a cookbook including he interviews and recipes from the folks of Rabun County that they so graciously shared with us.

We hope you enjoy learning more about the wonderful people who live here. The credit really goes to them. I thoroughly enjoyed my visits with them during the last three and a half years, renewing old friendships and making new friends.

When Tracy suggested a book signing, that provided an experience I never dreamed would be mine. Thank you Tracy and all of my friends at the "Laurel" for the confidence you have shown in me. We hope our book gives you much pleasure.

Most Sincerely,
Jean Emhart

MY GUESTS AND THEIR INTERVIEWS

Including recipes from the staff of The Georgia Mountain Laurel
Tracy McCoy   John Shivers   Dianne VanderHorst
Nikki McCall   Robin Welch
Sally Wilson   Linda & Trudy Crunkleton

Rabun's Laurel welcomes
Mrs. Jean Emhart and Rabun's Recipes

The following appeared in the June 2004 of Rabun's Laurel Magazine.

Rabun's Laurel is proud to introduce a new monthly column written by Jean Emhart of Clayton. Each month, beginning in July, Emhart will interview and feature a hometown cook and their favorite recipes. Think Barbara Walters meets Emeril or the Naked Chef right here on the page. She is excited about the new opportunity, as we are, and keeps adding to her list of those she wants to feature. Teasing our gastronomic desires might be a chili recipe from a local firehouse or a dessert to die for from a friend of hers. Rabun County has so man good cooks, Emhart calls the possibilities endless.

Emhart's son Steven folded newspapers for the Clayton Tribune while attending high school and that precipitated her writing. "I backed into a writing career," she said.

The paper was looking for someone to write of neighborhood events and the elder Emhart jumped at the chance. It evolved into a column called "Strictly for the Girls" in the 1960s. "I would give anything for the chance to write. I love writing and I love the interview process. It's so nice to get to sit down with people and learn about them," she said.

The one-day-a-week job at the Tribune lasted a few years until the homemaker pursued other interests as her son reached adulthood. The writing went on hiatus. Though she helped with keeping medical records at Rabun County Hospital, most locals remember her as Dr. Richard Turner's secretary, a position she held for 23 years.

Her husband's work led them to Rabun County. Harry Emhart was a dye chemist for James Lee's and Son (makers of Heavenly carpets), later purchased by Burlington Industries, with a plant in Rabun Gap, Georgia. Transferred here in 1958 from their origins in Pennsylvania, the couple fell in love with the place. "Harry was an avid golfer and we'd heard of the place as a wonderful spot in northeast Georgia where the climate allows playing almost year round. Then we fell in love with the south, the mountains, the scenery and most of all the people," she said.

They ping-ponged about due to job transfers for a while, then settled in Rabun County for good in 1971. Incredibly, in the same house they left. "I knelt down in a room of the house we were leaving in 1958 and asked the Lord to give it to the right family," Emhart said. "I never dreamed we'd be back."

She gives credit to the friends she's accumulated through the years in Rabun County as she copes with the loss of her husband a few years ago. Like most mothers, Emhart likes to brag of her family. Her son Steven became a National Merit finalist under the direction of Star Teacher Clayton Croom here. He then went on to graduate from Georgia Tech and went to the Officer's Training School of the Air Force. After an early out for education, he obtained a Master's Degree from the University of North Carolina. He and his wife Christene live in Kerry, North Carolina, near Raleigh. Jean Emhart has two grandchildren, Dustin and Cassandra, and one great-grandchild, Evangellan.

After respite, she's once again taken up the craft of writing she so enjoys, happy to add it to her list of things she likes to do. It joins music (she was formerly the organist for Clayton Baptist Church), reading (I frequent the library more than most"), walking for exercise, playing bridge with friends and traveling.

"I'm delighted to be a part of a magazine of such high caliber," she said. "It's fantastic that those two young girls (Janet Cummings and Marjorie Fielding, publishers) had such vision and were able to carry it out."

Whether it's the act of cooking or writing about it, Emhart says "When we love something, that's when it goes well."

by Tony Wheeler

Since purchasing the *Laurel* in 2006 and having the pleasure of getting to know Jean better, I have seen what pleasure she takes in doing our recipe column. The ever efficient "secreatary" in Jean makes working with her even more of a blessing. Always on time with her articles and with a list of interviews scheduled for the months ahead, she puts us all to shame when it comes to sticking to our deadline.

Jean Emhart is a gracious and kind woman and a dear friend to us all. We appreciate the wonderful work she has done and how well she represents our magazine. I hope that Jean will treasure this book as much as we treasure her.

Tracy McCoy

July, 2004

Across the table from

Di Wiggins

kitchen. This may be called one of their hobbies, as they have done this sort of thing before and are currently working on renovating their house in Hilton Head.

Di worked diligently on a cookbook compiled by the Wiley Presbyterian Church entitled Blended Blessings and is available in local stores. Di worked on other cookbooks in 1985, '90 and '95, and compiled a loose-leaf book of her own which she calls "Lady Di Easy Does It." This is interspersed with pictures and funny sayings along with her recipes. She shares many of these recipes with her friends at Christmas time. Now.... to the recipes:

Last week I had a delightful visit with Di Wiggins here in Clayton. We sat on her sun-porch which was surrounded on three sides by windows, giving the effect of being in a tree house. We enjoyed "Yummy Breakfast Rolls" with our coffee. Di gave us the recipe for this.

Di grew up in Marietta and "Wig" as her husband is called, grew up in Carrolton. They raised two sons and have two grandchildren, Trent and Savanna. They used to be tennis buffs; now their interest has turned to golf.

The Wiggins bought the A.I.D. Corporation in 1989. They make parts for the aircraft industry. The company was started by the Hub Lesley family whom many of you will remember. They also own Gap Manufacturing, which makes different types of metal enclosures. You can see their creation at the Whistle Stop Mall in Franklin, North Carolina, when you view the water wheel. They also make racks that hold wine casks for a local winery. Wig travels overseas on business and Di accompanies him on many of these trips. Di likes to collect cookbooks whenever she travels.

They moved here seven years ago and bought a condo in Sky Valley. Then they purchased a home in Bleckley Place two years later. They renovated it an built a lovely sun-porch and enlarged the

Sausage-Hash Brown Casserole

Note: This is my favorite new breakfast dish and the recipe is often requested.

2 lb. sausage
2 c. cheddar cheese, shredded
1 can cream of chicken soup
  (you may want to use the light)
1 1/2 c. sour cream
4 oz. French onion dip
1 c. onion, chopped (I use less)
Salt and pepper to taste
1 (30 oz.) pkg. hash brown potatoes,
  shredded
3 eggs

Cook sausage until brown. Drain well. Combine cheese, chicken soup, sour cream, onion dip, onion, and eggs. Fold in hash browns and mix well. Spread half of potato mixture in 9x13 inch greased baking dish. Spread half of the browned sausage over hash browns. Repeat hash browns,
Bake at 375 degrees for about an hour or until casserole is golden brown.

Baked Cheese Grits

Note: Our grown sons still love this dish; it re-heats beautifully)

4 c. water
1 c. quick grits
1 c. milk
1 tsp. salt
1 stick butter
4 eggs, slightly beaten
1 (6 oz.) Kraft Garlic Cheese Roll
   (available at Piggly Wiggly)
1/2 c. grated cheese

Cook grits according to package directions. Add cheese roll and stir until melted. Add stick of butter and stir until melted. Add milk and eggs and stir. Pour into greased casserole and bake 1 hour at 350 degrees. After an hour, sprinkle grated cheese on top and return to oven for 5 minutes.

Yummy Breakfast Rolls

Note: Yum-m-m-m-y! These are great for brunch and some friends have served it as dessert.

2 cans crescent rolls
16 oz. cream cheese (may be light)
1 1/4 c. sugar
1 tbsp. vanilla
1 tbsp. cinnamon
1 stick margarine, melted

Unroll 1 can of crescent rolls into bottom of 13x9x2 inch pan. Don't press seams together! Mix cream cheese with 1 cup of sugar and vanilla; spread over rolls. Place second can of rolls on top. Pour melted butter or margarine on top: then top with mixture of 1/4 cup sugar and cinnamon. Bake for 30 minutes at 350 deg.

Creamy Egg Salad

Note: I have served this as a spread for crackers or as a sandwich filling. Since raw onions isn't a favorite of mine, I substitute green olives. This recipe is easily halved.

2 (8 oz.) pkgs. cream cheese, softened
1/2 c. mayonnaise
1 tsp. ground mustard
1/2 tsp. paprika
1/2 tsp. salt
8 hard cooked eggs, chopped (I put in 10)
1 medium onion, chopped or green olives to taste
Croissants or sandwich rolls, optional
Lettuce leaves, optional

In a mixing bowl, beat cream cheese, mayonnaise, mustard, paprika and salt. Stir in eggs and onion. Serve on Croissants with lettuce, if desired. Yield: about 5 cups

Apple Dumplings

Note: this is my favorite dessert to make for people as a "thinking of you" sweet treat. You may reheat each dumpling as wanted in the microwave and ice cream is great with them.

1 c. sugar
1 c. water
1 stick butter, divided
1/2 tsp. cinnamon
1/2 tsp. nutmeg
1 (8 oz.) can of refrigerated
   crescent dinner rolls
1 (20 oz.) can apple pie filling
Cinnamon, sugar and nutmeg to sprinkle

Preheat oven to 350 deg. In medium saucepan combine sugar, water, 5 1/2 tbsp. butter, cinnamon and nutmeg. Bring to boil; set aside. Separate dinner rolls and roll thin. Spoon 2 tbsp. of pie filling into middle of each piece of dough. Fold over and seal edges. Place in shallow baking dish. Sprinkle with a little cinnamon, sugar and nutmeg, Dot with remaining butter, pour sugar mixture over dumplings. Bake 30 minutes or until brown, basting often. Yield: 8 dumplings

Across the table from

Pete Marziliano

From the moment I drove into the driveway of the Marziliano's home in Tiger, I felt at home. As we entered their home, a delicious aroma came from the kitchen, proof I was in the home of people who loved food.

Linda and Pete both attended the University of Georgia. Their studies took them to the same hall, but they never met. Pete thinks this was for the best as he was the hippie type and Linda was quite the opposite.

1971 found them both in Savannah, Georgia, as Cooperative Extension Agents. My son would say this was a Godincidence rather than a coincidence. Linda was in the food and Nutrition area, while Pete was in the area of agriculture. Both worked with the 4-H program. Pete was then promoted to Habersham County as their County Extension Agent in 1976. Linda taught school at Habersham Central, then at N.E. Georgia Tech. Evidently the hippie and the proper gal saw something more in each other than just appearance.

After marrying, they moved to Habersham County and had two children, a girl named Lauren and a boy they named Jonathan. Pete received another promotion as Rabun County's Extension Agent and Director in 1985. They built their home in Tiger at that time. Pete is quoted as saying, "I did what Sherman couldn't do; I took your land and took your women." Pete hails from New York and Linda is from Dublin, Georgia.

While in Habersham County, Pete penned a column entitled "Yankee Peddler," writing for The Anderson Independent, The Gainesville Times and The Clayton Tribune. A friend has suggested that Pete put these articles in book form and after reading several of them, I agree. Pete has a good sense of humor along with his knowledge. I remember one time I called and asked him when I should trim back my nandina and he answered, "When Georgia Tech wins a football game." He is a devoted UGA fan and we were Tech fans. Pete is now retired and enjoys restor-

ing antiques, and works mainly with dealers. He does everything by hand, the stripping, finishing, etc., as evidenced by furniture in their home. You run your hand over the finish and realize the love of the work that goes into these pieces.

He enjoys back-packing and mountain climbing. He works with the youth of the church on Wednesday nights and takes them on many trips. One can see he chooses to spend his retirement years in a useful and rewarding way.

Linda is employed by the Rabun County Board of Education as School Nutrition director. Her office is in Mountain City and she visits all public schools, working with cafeteria managers to prepare menus, etc. She purchases the food for the school system, prepares the budget along with free reduced applications. So, one can see just how complex her job is.

It is interesting to note that Linda was brought to Rabun County by her physician father and her mother when she was 2 1/2 months old. Her father built a cabin on Lake Burton which they enjoy today.

Then I found out what the delicious aroma was coming from the kitchen. We all sat around the table and enjoyed a Buttermilk Pie that Linda prepared. I asked if Linda was going to supply me with recipes and she informed me that Pete was the chief cook and bottle washer. Pete supplied the recipes for us today. As his father was Italian and his mother German, these recipes reflect both cultures.

Cavollin Agrodolce
(Cabbage in a Sweet & Sour Sauce)
This is a favorite in our family and adds and interesting taste to cabbage.

1 1/2 pounds of cabbage,
  cut into 1/4 inch strips
3 large tomatoes, chopped
1/2 cup thinly sliced onions
1 T Olive Oil
2 T Wine Vinegar
2 tsp. salt
1 T sugar
Dash of Pepper

Heat oil and add onions. Cook over a moderate heat, stirring, until onions are transparent. Add the cabbage, tomatoes, vinegar, salt and the dash of pepper. Simmer uncovered until cabbage is tender. Stir in sugar and cook for about 1-2 minutes more. Serve hot.

Broiled Eggplant Rounds

One eggplant (you may use more if you are having company or the dish is being used as an appetizer. This dish is an excellent appetizer or it can be used as one of the vegetables in your meal.)

Pesto
Fat-free Feta Cheese
Olive Oil
Salt and Pepper
Pine Nuts

Slice the eggplant into rounds about 1/2 to 3/4 inches thick. You can leave the skin on but it will be somewhat chewy. Lay the rounds on a baking tray, sprinkling both sides of the rounds with salt (eggplant may have a slightly bitter taste that the salt removes), and let stand for 30 minutes. Blot dry. Coat both sides with olive oil and add salt and pepper if desired. I find that the residue of the salt used to remove any bitterness is enough for our tastes, so don't add any more. Broil the eggplant rounds about 4 inches from the heat until browned, usually less than 10 minutes. Turn the rounds and broil the other side. When done, I put some pesto, some roasted pine nuts and some fat-free Feta cheese on top, and return to the broiler until the cheese starts to melt. Remove and serve immediately.

This might be a good time to mention that I have a bad habit of modifying recipes. In the cabbage dish, I may add more onion, less tomato, or even less cabbage, depending on what is in the pantry. Because of a fairly recent heart attack and bypass surgery, I now add very little salt, cook with olive or canola oil and use mostly fat-free dairy products. Non fat-free dairy products taste better and if your diet allows it, use them. I have genetically high cholesterol, which is controlled with drugs and diet. We mostly eat chicken, fish and venison. Venison is low fat, organic and gives me another excuse to hunt in the fall.

The last recipe is one we have used for years. It is an Italian Double Meat Loaf recipe that started off with beef and was modified to be used with ground venison. Like most of my recipes, I modify it as I go along and the mood to add different things strikes me.

Italian Double Meat Loaf

2 pounds of ground venison (or beef,
  or even turkey)
1 1/2 cups of Italian Bread Crumbs
2 eggs
1 tsp. garlic salt
1/8 tsp. pepper
1/2 cup grated Parmesan cheese
1/2 cup water

In a metal bowl, mix the meat and the bread crumbs, Add the eggs and the water. Mix thoroughly. Add the cheese and the other ingredients. If the mixture appears too loose, add a little more bread crumbs, but be conservative. A little will thicken the mixture quickly. Form the mixture into two oval loaves and place in a 13x9x2 inch baking dish. At this point I may sprinkle the tops of the loaves with Cayenne Pepper and Paprika for a little extra zest. Bake uncovered at 350 degrees for 1 hour. This recipe makes a fairly firm, tasty meat loaf. One loaf will serve 4 with some left over, and the second meat loaf can be frozen for later use. If you like a moister loaf, you can add 1/4 cup of Steak Seasoning mixed with 1/2 cup of water to the baking dish.

Across the table from

Mary Cole & Barbara Moran

First you buy a chandelier and then you build a house around it. That is what May Cole and Barbara Moran did up on Walnut Mountain. Now let's learn more about these two most interesting ladies.

Mary grew up in Michigan and attended Nursing School at Butterworth Hospital in Grand Rapids. She practiced psychiatric nursing for one year and then decided to join the Air Force. She was stationed in Florida, and in Alaska before it became a state. Then she went to Japan and England. Mary retired after 24 years of service

Barbara grew up in Woonsocket, Rhode Island. She attended nursing school in Milford, Mass. She chose a career as a flight attendant with Western Airlines in Denver, Colorado. After four years she decided to go back into nursing and joined the Air Force. In that way she could fly and practice nursing at the same time. She was stationed in Texas, Michigan, New York and Florida, then overseas in Japan and Morocco. Barbara retired after 20 years of service.

These two nurses met while serving in Japan and formed a lasting friendship. After retirement, they bought and ran a farm in Dade City, Florida, where they raised sheep and Gertrudis cattle which were bred on the King Ranch in Texas. They are large, russet-haired animals, and come from South America. They also raised a pig each year for their own use, along with chickens and lambs. They were fond of green peppers and devoted a large area to this purpose.

Several years ago, a friend came to Mary and asked if she would like to use a cabin that he had reserved for several years running. The cabin was on top of Black Rock Mountain here in Rabun County. She and Barbara decided this would be a nice change of scenery and took him up on his offer. Once the ladies spent some time here in our mountains, they made reservations to come back in the fall to see the changing leaves. Well, they were hooked! They saw an advertisement for a shell of a house with a porch. A local contractor finished the house for them and they began spending summers here while neighbors took care of the farm. They eventually sold the farm and built a house in another part of Florida, but they were so taken with the mountains, the climate and the people, that they sold the house and moved permanently to Georgia.

Their hobbies include the traditional art form of virgin wool rug hooking (this is different from the more modern rug latching) and traveling. One can admire many beautiful hand hooked rugs in their house today which are heirlooms. They began classes under the instruction of Nomi Stopher when she held classes at the public library, then later in her own home. This is where I met these ladies. Their travels have taken them to Greece, Ireland, Australia, New Zealand, Portugal, France, Germany, Austria, Holland, Singapore, Korea and all of the Czech countries.

Finally, it was time to build a house around their beloved chandelier. They now live on Walnut Mountain near Rabun Gap, and are surrounded by their mementos from all over the world and their beloved rugs. Oddly enough they found a matching, smaller chandelier at a flea market. Needless to say, we had a most interesting conversation around the dining room table, under the coveted chandelier. The stories they tell of their trips are both amusing and informative. Barbara is the cook in the household and she prepared the following lunch for us. Now you can enjoy it too

Old Fashioned Blueberry Muffins

2 cups all-purpose flour
2/3 cup sugar
1 tbsp. baking powder
1/2 tsp. salt
1/2 tsp. nutmeg
2 eggs, beaten
1/2 cup milk
1/2 cup melted margarine
1/4 cup toasted almonds
1 tbsp. sugar
1 1/2 cups blueberries

Combine flour, sugar, baking powder, salt, nutmeg. Reserve 1 tbsp. of the flour mix to toss with blueberries. Make well in center. Combine eggs, milk and butter. Add to dry ingredients. Stir only until moist. Toss berries with remaining flour mix. Stir into batter. Spoon into greased muffin tins 1/3 full. Sprinkle with almonds and sugar. Bake at 400 degrees for 15-18 minutes. Makes 18 muffins.

Sauteed Shrimp with Tomatoes, Olives and Feta

1/2 cup olive oil
6 cloves garlic, chopped
2 tbsp. dried oregano
3 lbs. uncooked medium shrimp,
    peeled & de-veined
3/4 cup quartered pitted Kalamata olives
    (4 oz.)
3/4 lb. plum tomatoes, seeded & chopped
1/2 cup chopped fresh basil
1 1/2 cups crumbled Feta cheese (7 oz.)

Heat oil in heavy skillet over high heat. Add garlic and oregano. Stir. Add shrimp and olives. Sautee 3 minutes. Add tomatoes and chopped basil. Stir. Season with salt and pepper. Sprinkle with Feta. Serve over lettuce.

Stuffed Peach Halves

4 medium peaches, peeled, halved
    and seeded
1 tbsp. lemon juice
2 tbsp. unsweetened flaked toasted coconut
2 tbsp. raisins
2 tbsp. chopped toasted almonds
1/2 tsp. lemon rind grated
1/2 tsp. ground cinnamon
2 tbsp. vanilla lowfat yogurt
2 tsp. honey
1 tsp. vanilla extract

Coat peach halves with lemon juice. Combine remaining ingredients and stir well. Spoon 1 tbsp. of mix into cavity of each peach half. Chill. Makes 8 servings.

Across the table from

Don & Penny Melton

Since coming to Rabun County I have always admired and coveted the view from the south of Bridge Creek Road, which overlooks the distant mountains. This property belonged to Janie P. Taylor's mother. You are all familiar with Janie's endearing articles in Rabun's Laurel. This was the view I enjoyed as I parked in Penny & Don Melton's driveway. I have known Penny and Don for many years and welcomed the opportunity to visit with them.

Penny and Don both grew up in Mulberry, Florida. Don was sent to military school in Barnesville, Georgia from 1947 until 1951. Upon graduation, he joined the Navy in 1952 and was discharged in 1956. He attended the University of Florida and was a Gator fan. Penny attended Florida State and was a Seminole fan. Penny finally converted Don to her side. Since living in Georgia, Don has become a Bulldog fan rivaling my Yellow Jackets.

Penny and Don started dating after Don's discharge from the Navy and married in 1957. They began vacationing in Waynesville, North Carolina, where they developed an interest in antiques, mostly primitives, by attending auctions. One year they decided to stay at the Dillard House. The found this area to be just what they were looking for and bought a summer home in Mountain City, but continued attending auctions in Winston-Salem. This evolved into an antique business they started on Highway 441 in Mountain City. They decided to move here permanently and built a house on the side of a mountain on Black's Creek Road.

Always seeking out new adventures, they gave up the antique business and started Penny's Garden in 1987. There was a small cabin on the property, which they converted into a little shop where they sold herbs, jellies, vinegars, flowers, and wreaths. I wonder just how many of you visited this garden and its little shop. I know I did. This garden remained open until 1999 when they decided to sell it and retire.

Penny tells me that she starts her herbs in pots and then transplants them into a garden spot. They like good drainage so mix a little gravel in with the soil. The great thing about growing herbs, is that they return each year and do not have to be fertilized. You may also grow them in pots if this is more convenient for you. Her favorite is basil, but she also has success with chives and rosemary.

You can freeze your herbs in baggies. I also read that you may chop them up, freeze them in ice cubes trays and just plop the cube into your cooking for that much desired flavor.

Speaking of the herb rosemary, as we were chatting, I found two big eyes staring at me without a blink, sizing me up. This was the family cat perched on the edge of the coffee table with her paws hanging over. This kitty appeared at Penny's garden the day after Christmas one year and has lived with her now six or seven years. It always amazes me how these animals know which family to choose. As she grew, Penny and Don noticed that she kept rubbing up against the rosemary bush, so she was named Rosemary. This didn't seem to fit her temperament, so they shortened it to Rosie. I hope Rosie approved of my visit.

As we talked in their lovely family room, Don was busy hooking a runner for their antique dining room table. It is patterned after a Navaho blanket in shades of tan, brown, white and black. Don attends hooking classes under the direction of Mary Williamson. He has also hooked a lovely rug for their foyer and a rendition of a Frank Lloyd Wright stained glass design.

Thank you Penny and Don for a most delightful afternoon in which we talked about old times and new times, and shared Penny's love of cooking with herbs.

Here are some of Penny's favorite recipes for us to enjoy.

Pesto

2 cups of firmly packed fresh basil leaves
1/2 cup of pine nuts
3 cloves of peeled garlic
3/4 cup of freshly grated Parmesan cheese
2 cups of olive oil

Blend basil, nuts and garlic in food processor until pureed. Blend in cheese and slowly add oil while blending on low speed. Serve immediately or add a thin layer of olive oil and refrigerate. This can be frozen in small portions. Serve on pasta, baked potatoes, broiled fish, tomatoes, etc.

Boursin-type Cheese

1 lb. cream cheese, softened
1/2 lb. butter, softened
1 tsp. mashed garlic
1 1/2 Tbsp. chopped sweet marjoram
1 1/2 Tbsp. chopped chives
1 Tbsp. chopped basil
1 tsp. thyme
1 Tbsp. chopped parsley
1 1/2 tsp. salt
1/4 tsp. white pepper

You may substitute other herbs or even omit some, but you MUST USE FRESH BASIL. (I usually omit marjoram because I have trouble growing it.) Beat cheese and butter together. Add garlic and mix well. Add herbs, salt, and pepper. Chill slightly and form into logs or balls. Wrap in plastic wrap and refrigerate or freeze. Serve with crackers or Melba toast.

Rosemary Pecans

1 Tbsp. melted butter
1 Tbsp. finely chopped fresh rosemary
1/2 tsp. salt
1/4 tsp. paprika
1 cup pecan halves

Mix butter and seasonings together in a shallow baking pan. Add nuts, turning them in a mixture to coat. Heat for 7-10 minutes in a 350 degree oven, stirring occasionally. Nuts will become crisp as they cool.

November, 2004

Don & Kathleen Arbitter

*N*ovember brings to mind long walks in your favorite snugly sweater, enjoying views you can see now that the leaves are off the trees, the smell of a wood burning fireplace and more importantly, Thanksgiving. This is a time to pause and reflect on the many blessings God has bestowed on each of us. With this in mind, I chose a family whose lives revolve around God and family, along with many traditions. If you do not have family traditions, start one or two this year to be carried on by your family year after year.

Kathleen and I sat on her deck overlooking Lake Burton on a beautiful September morning. We enjoyed Scotch Shortbread with our coffee while we chatted. Kathleen and Don were brought up in Michigan, about 60 miles apart. Kathleen went to Wheaton College in Wheaton, Illinois while Don chose to attend Houghton College in upstate New York.

Don's work was closing in Brooklyn, New York. He traveled south in the Smokies on his way to Florida the summer of 1957. It was during that trip down Highway 441 that he passed Rabun Gap Nacoochee School and remembered he had applied for a job there. On a subsequent trip north to Boston, Dr. Karl Anderson stopped by Kahlman Home for Children in Brooklyn, New York where Don was working and asked him if he was interested in accepting the Guidance Counselor's position at RGNS and in 1958 Don arrived at RGNS in Rabun Gap.

In 1962 both Kathleen and Don signed up for a trip to Israel sponsored by Wheaton College. They met that December in Jerusalem! This is what I call a "God-incidence." When they returned to their respective professions, they continued their new found friendship by correspondence. Kathleen came to Rabun Gap to visit in 1964. Don introduced her to Dr. Anderson who offered her the position of Director of Special Education. Kathleen moved to RGNS in 1964 where she began her new job and lived in the girls dormitory assisting the housemother with evening study time and directed the InterSchool Christian Fellowship for the teenagers (ISCF is the High School counterpart of InterVarsity). Somewhere along the line, the story was related to me that Don "proposed" to Kathleen while walking the corn fields on RGNS campus, looking for arrowheads!! They were married in June, 1965.

The lived on campus from 1965 until 1992. They have two children, Ruth was born in 1966 and now resides in Flowery Branch with her husband Paul Ebbs who is Manager of the new Boggs Mountain Animal Shelter here in Rabun County. They have a two year old daughter, Lydia. Don and Kathleen's son, Stephen was born in 1968. He is a veterinarian of Rabun Animal Hospital in Mountain City. He is married to Jennifer Cathey who is news director with Channel 32 in Toccoa. They have a two year old son named Mark. The two little cousins enjoy playing together very much.

After Don's retirement they built their dream house on Lake Burton. They are both very active in the work at Clayton Baptist Church teaching adult Sunday school classes, singing in the choir, etc. Kathleen began Kidz Praiz, a children's worship service. Kathleen and Don continue to substitute in the school system and Don is associated with Century 21 Poss Realty.

The Arbitters have always spent Thanksgiving at home in Rabun County. When the children were growing up, their tradition was to enjoy a big brunch, and while the turkey was baking, they would go out in the fields and find a Christmas tree and greens. They came home an decorated the tree and house while the delicious odors permeated from the kitchen. Now with their extended family, the past few years Don and Kathleen have had brunch in Flowery Branch with Ruth, Paul and family. Stephen and Jennifer join them after running in the Atlanta Road Race! Later in the day, they join Stephen Jennifer and

Mark at Frank and Brenda Cathey's home in Mountain City.

Then it was time to drink some tea with leaves brought from Don and Kathleen's trip to China and we enjoyed the coconut cranberry bars as given in Kathleen's recipes. It is obvious that the Arbitters would be comfortable anywhere in the world. Are we not fortunate they have chosen Rabun County as their home.

Corn Bake

3 eggs, slightly beaten
1 (8 1/2 oz.) package corn muffin mix
1 (8 oz.) can cream style corn
2 (16 oz.) cans whole kernel corn, drained
1 cup sour cream
1/2 cup melted butter
1 (4 oz.) can green chillies, chopped
1 cup cheddar cheese, shredded

Preheat oven to 350 degrees. Combine all ingredients except the cheese. Bake 1 hour. Spread cheese on top and bake 15 more minutes. Serves 8-10

Holiday Cranberry Salad

3 packages raspberry jello
1 quart cranberries
2 oranges, peel and pulp
2 apples, peel and pulp
1 large can crushed pineapple (drained)
2 cups sugar
Nuts optional

Prepare jello according to package directions, using pineapple juice as part of the liquid. Chill until consistency of unbeaten egg whites. Grind oranges, apples, cranberries. Add sugar. Allow sugar to dissolve. Add pineapple. Combine the fruit mixture with jello./ Pour into mold or large oblong dish
*This is a large recipe, but keeps well for holiday dining!

Thanksgiving Brunch Caramel-Orange Ring

1 tablespoon butter, softened
2 tablespoons chopped nuts
1 cup firmly packed brown sugar
1/2 teaspoon cinnamon
2 10 oz. cans refrigerated buttermilk
    flaky biscuits
1/2 cup butter, melted

Preheat oven to 350 degrees. Grease 12 cup bundt pan with 1 tablespoon butter. Place teaspoonfuls of orange marmalade in pan. Sprinkle with nuts. In small bowl combine brown sugar and cinnamon. Mix well, set aside. Separate biscuits. Dip biscuits in melted butter, then sugar mixture. Stand biscuits on edge in pan, spacing evenly. Sprinkle with remaining sugar mixture and drizzle with remaining butter. Bake near center of oven for 30-40 minutes or until brown. Cool upright in pan for 5 minutes, invert onto serving plate. Yield: 6-8 servings.

Coconut Cranberry Bars

1 1/2 cups graham cracker crumbs
1/2 cup butter, melted
    Spray Pam into 9x11 inch pan. Mix and press graham cracker mixture into pan

1 1/2 cups white chocolate chips
1 1/2 cups dried cranberries
1 14 oz. can sweetened condensed milk
1 cup coconut
1 cup chopped pecans
    Mix and gently spread over crust. Bake at 350 degrees for 25-28 minutes until edges are golden brown.
    **These holiday bars keep very well sealed tightly in Tupperware.

December, 2004

Across the table from

Nora Findley

I have been friends with Nora Findley for many years, having first met her when she visited the office and the hospital settings. She was always so friendly and brought wonderful goodies for us to enjoy. I have asked Nora to tell you more about her background, so here are her words:

I was born in Baldwin, New York. My mother didn't have the patience to teach her five girls to cook or bake, so I taught myself from cookbooks. I lived in the north for 27 years and moved to Rabun County when Dr. Findley went to work for Dr. Turner. We thought this was a wonderful place to raise our children. Emily is now 19 and is a freshman at UGA. Ben is 16 and a junior at RGNS. I loved living at the foot of Tiger Mountain, and I have decided that I want my ashes scattered on top of this mountain.

I now work 7:00 a.m. until 7:00 p.m. at Mountain View Nursing Home as a registered nurse. I also have a healing business out of my office at home during the week. I will have been an RN for 30 years this December. I live in Mountain City with my friend Van, my son Ben, two dogs, and three cats.

I prefer casual entertaining when each guests brings a part of the meal. My favorite party would be all hors d'oeuvres. Busy people don't have time to spend making complicated dishes, unless that is a joy and a pleasure that they budget time for. I see cooking and baking as a creative outlet; no different than making music, crafts, painting, or sculpture. Sharing food made with the intention of love is a sacred and joyful pastime - necessary for good health.

Now to the recipes:

Pickle-Ham Christmas Trees

Thinly-sliced deli ham
Dill pickle spears
Whipped cream cheese
 (easier to spread on ham)
Toothpicks

Open piece of ham and spread with cream cheese, thinly and evenly. Lay pickle spear along side and roll up. Cut into 1 1/2 inch pieces and lay them on their sides, securing at loose end with a toothpick. You may add small cube of cheese or pepperoni for a 'trunk' at the toothpick site.

Cream Cheese and Olive Trees

16 oz. cream cheese softened
 (or whipped cream cheese)
Jar of pimento-stuffed olives, quartered
Optional - jar of whole pickles or gherkins,
 sliced to 3/4 inch pieces
Loaf of party rye, four-inch square bread

Mix cream cheese and olives. Make sandwiches using the small square bread (may use larger bread cut smaller, If you wish). Cut each sandwich diagonally making small triangles.

Nora's Locally Famous Shrimp Dip

8 oz. Cream cheese
1 tbsp. Mayonnaise
1 tbsp. Worcestershire sauce
1 tbsp. Lemon juice
Grated small onion
Seafood cocktail sauce
Small Shrimp
Dried parsley
Townhouse crackers

Beat together the first five ingredients and spread on a dinner plate. Over cream cheese layer, spread a thin layer of seafood cocktail sauce. Crumble or arrange small shrimp over this. Crumble dried parsley on top and chill. Serve with Town House Christmas-shape crackers (or any Ritz-type cracker).

Easy Work Day Spread

(If your hostess will lend you a plate and knife, you can even run to the store on your way to the party.)

8 oz. block of cream cheese, Green and red pepper jelly (hard to find outside the south)

Any type of buttery crackers. Lay cream cheese on a Christmassy plate. Spoon jellies over the top. Arrange crackers all around and serve with a spreading knife.

Pesto Pizza Wedges

One large pizza crust or several small ones
Pesto
Sun-dried tomatoes
Crumbled feta

Follow directions related to its baking. Spread with pesto (preferably homemade) instead of red sauce. Place marinated sun-dried tomatoes and crumbled feta cheese over pesto. Add anything else that sounds good, stuffed green olives, black olives, herbs, mushrooms, etc. Bake and cool. Cut into thin wedges and serve on a tray.

Linda's Rum Cake
From Linda Angel

I yellow butter recipe cake mix
1 pkg. vanilla instant pudding
1/2 c. oil
4 eggs
1/2 c. cold water
1/2 c. 81 proof dark rum

Glaze
1 stick butter
1/4 c. water
1 c. sugar
1/2 c. rum
Pecans

Mix cake mix according to box directions, (be sure to include 1 stick butter, as mix calls for), add pudding mix and blend well, pour into a bundt pan coated with baking spray and lined with the pecans (chopped makes the cake easier to slice). Bake 1 hour at 325.

For Glaze: In a saucepan, place butter, sugar and water. Bring to boil, let boil for 5 minutes. Remove from heat. Add rum. Pour over warm cake (you may want to punch holes in cake with a fork to let glaze drizzle in).

Cooking Tip: Prepare what you need before you start. It's how the pros do it and it simplifies the process when you are scrambling to put it all together.

Snack Shack Restaurant Chili
From Linda Angel & Trudy Crunkleton

This was given to me by Amos Gillespie who got it from the original owner of the Snack Shack Restaurant in Clayton.

1 lb. lean ground beef
Chopped onions
1 (6 oz.) can tomato paste
Salt & pepper to taste
Dash garlic powder
Dash Tabasco
Dash Worcestershire
2 tbsps. chili powder

Brown beef in skillet, add chopped onions. When nearly done, drain grease in colander and return to skillet. Add tomato paste and salt and pepper to taste. Add garlic powder, Tabasco, Worcestershire and chili powder. Simmer 1 hour.

Meemaw's Squash Casserole
From Linda Angel

This recipe was probably one of the first squash casserole recipes. It is Melba Dotson's own recipe and has been published in the Georgia Federation of Women's Club Cook Books. She wrote the recipe down for her daughters & granddaughters

3 lbs. fresh squash
1 large onion, chopped
2 c. crushed cornbread
Ritz crackers or Saltines
1/2 to 3/4 lb. grated sharp Cheddar
1 stick butter
1 c. milk
2 tsp. salt
11/2 tsp. white pepper
2 eggs, beaten
1 c. crushed potato chips

Slice squash thin, don't peel; stew until just tender; drain. Butter casserole dish, layer squash, cracker crumbs, cheese and onions, alternating layers; melt butter, mix with milk, eggs, salt and pepper. Pour over squash mixture and let sit for 20 minutes. Bake at 350 for 20 to 25 minutes. Spread remaining cheese and crushed potato chips and bake for 3-4 minutes more.

Cooking Measurement Equivalents

1 tablespoon (tbsp) = 3 teaspoons (tsp)
1/16 cup = 1 tablespoon
1/8 cup = 2 tablespoons
1/6 cup = 2 tablespoons + 2 teaspoons
1/4 cup = 4 tablespoons
1/3 cup = 5 tablespoons + 1 teaspoon
3/8 cup = 6 tablespoons
1/2 cup = 8 tablespoons
2/3 cup = 10 tablespoons + 2 teaspoons
3/4 cup = 12 tablespoons
1 cup = 48 teaspoons
1 cup = 16 tablespoons
8 fluid ounces (fl oz) = 1 cup
1 pint (pt) = 2 cups
1 quart (qt) = 2 pints
4 cups = 1 quart
1 gallon (gal) = 4 quarts
16 ounces (oz) = 1 pound (lb)

A "dash" is a small amount of an ingredient, usually about 1/16 of a teaspoon.

U.S. to Metric

1/4 cup = 60 milliliters
1/2 cup = 120 milliliters
1 cup = 230 milliliters
1 1/4 cups = 300 milliliters
1 1/2 cups = 360 milliliters
2 cups 460 = milliliters
2 1/2 cups = 600 milliliters
3 cups = 700 milliliters
4 cups (1 quart) = .95 liter
1.06 quarts = 1 liter
4 quarts (1 gal) = 3.8 liters

January, 2005

Alliene Jones

Alliene Jones and I became acquainted through the Pilot Club of Clayton as charter members many years ago. From this association, stemmed the Lunch Bunch, a group of about eight women who meet once a month to have lunch in the various local restaurants and to enjoy each other's company. This is the story as told to me by my friend, Alliene Smith Jones.

The Red Family High Chair: The only road to eastern Rabun County was a wagon road on the eastern boundary of her grandparents' property in the Wolf Creek community that provided access from western South Carolina to eastern North Carolina and to the lower part of Georgia. Many wagon loads of apples, cabbages, and other forms of produce were transported for sale in the lower counties of the state. This is how the community known as Camp Creek received its name. There was a nice level area with good spring water for people to use. They camped overnight when passing through. The red chair was found on this road near the gate to my grandmother's home. It was assumed that family was moving with a wagon load of possessions and that the chair fell off the wagon. The people were long gone down the road by then. It was handmade and three generations of our family used it.

The nearest post office was at Tallulah Falls where my grandparents rode by buggy to pick up their mail and shop at Calvoe Lee's General Merchandise Store where you could purchase anything you needed from rock candy to horse collars. There was a grist mill within a mile or so from our home, as the crow flies, on the horse trail where I rode many times with my father on our horse named Lucy, with a sack of corn or oats to be ground into meal or flour.

After the Tallulah Falls railroad was extended to Franklin, NC., the Lakes Burton, Seed and Rabun dams were built. My father was the only child left to farm. He walked six or seven miles and worked on the Mathis dam. He hewed crossties,

worked at the blacksmith shop and helped with the other work for my grandmother. He married a school teacher named Flora West and added a bedroom and screened in the back porch to my grandmother's log house where I was born. Our family doctor, Dr. James Green, came by buggy and stayed with my aunt and my father until I entered this world. At this time, there was one telephone within a five mile horseback ride that was provided by the U.S. Forest Service and used by all the community for emergencies, such as calling the doctor who practiced with Dr. J.C. Dover in Clayton.

When the cold weather came there was the butchering of hogs, beef and goats. We had a log smoke house where the hams and middlings (fat back and streak of lean) were salted and cured. Beef sides were hung for curing. We did not have a cellar and potatoes were bedded down and covered to prevent freezing. Cabbages, turnips, beets and carrots were bedded outside, covered and mulched with straw for winter use. We strung green beans, called "leather britches" to dry. We hulled peas and shelled corn to supplement our winter menus. We also dried apples and figs. As the butchering was done by the men, the ladies ground sausage, made "hogs-head cheese" (souse meat), liver mush and sliced what we now call pork chops. The bone was cut away and we ate fresh tenderloin for breakfast and carried it in our lunch boxes to school. Yeast bread was a treat and eggs were traded at the grocery store for "loaf bread".

We had cows, sweet milk, cream, buttermilk and butter, which we churned and worked out the water to make a beautiful round yellow mold of butter with a rose on top. These were kept fresh in a springhouse at the base of the hill and we toted water to the house. We were poor and didn't know it; we were happy and did know it, but I wish not for the "good old days". The chair is a happy memory of my father who glued it, 'C' clamped it together and sanded and stained it red to preserve it in a very usable condition for another generation to use when visiting. The children were tied in it with an old towel or piece of worn out sheet. They ate from the table as there was no tray attached to it. The story is a tribute to the love of our land and my ancestors.

Now to the recipes:

Buttermilk Cake Filling

The following recipe is from my "The Rumford Complete Cook Book". I was able to get this through labels my mother had saved from the coupons on the Rumford baking powder cans. I was in about the 5th grade when my mother dictated this recipe for Buttermilk Cake Filling and is written exactly copied back then. This will frost or fill 2 layers of a 9' cake but needs to be doubled if frosting the outside. Keep in mind that sugar was a cash purchase and most cakes were filled only on top and in the middle of the layers.

1 cup sugar, 1/2 cup buttermilk, 1/2 tsp. soda, 1/2 cup butter, 1/2 nutmeats if desired. Dissolve soda in buttermilk, add sugar and butter, mix thoroughly and cook stirring constantly when syrup forms a soft ball by dropping in cold water remove from the fire add nutmeats and beat till cool enough to spread have layers cool.

Note: lack of punctuation, etc., but this is exactly as I wrote it as my mother dictated it to me.

Salsa

We ate this with our dried peas particularly, and we called it "doing".

1 medium sized tomato per serving diced. We did not waste or discard the seeds and juice as they provided fiber.

1 small hot green pepper (we did not have jalapeno peppers), chopped as fine as possible.

1 small to medium onion, chopped. The size depended on how hot the onion was and to your taste

1 TB. vinegar, again to taste

a few pieces of finely chopped green pepper

1 pinch salt

2 tsp. sugar or more to taste

All of the above were mixed together in a non-aluminum container and allowed to marinate as long as possible before serving to top black-eyed peas, greens, beans, meat loaf or whatever your taste desired. Every cook preparing this dish tasted, added to or adjusted to her own taste.

Potato Biscuits

This is a good way to use left over mashed potatoes.

1 cup cooked potatoes

1 & 1/2 cups plain flour

2 level tsp. Rumford Baking Powder

1/2 level tsp. salt

1/4 cup shortening

1 egg

about 3/4 cups of milk

Boil and mash potatoes, making sure there are no lumps. Sift flour, salt and baking powder, add the potatoes and cut in the shortening with tines of fork, biscuit cutter or another instrument that will reduce the mixture to a course texture. Mix to a light dough with the egg and milk. Roll out a little thinner than ordinary biscuits and bake in a hot oven. Serve as soon as done.

For those of you who do not know what a hot oven is, it is between 425 and 450 degrees. Bake for 10-12 minutes or until browned to your liking. When this cookbook was published there were very few ovens with thermostats to control the temperature. Women, including my mother baked many of these on an iron wood range and you got smart enough to judge the temperature with your hand.

February, 2005

Inger Smith

*D*o you have a special place you like to go - a friendly place where you are made to feel welcome? Such a place for me is Inger's. I love to have lunch there with friends and enjoy the delights Inger has to offer. I call this my happy place! Many of you probably read the Restaurant Review in Rabun's Laurel, but I wanted an up close and personal interview with Inger. We sat over hot tea and almond cookies, Inger's latest, and they were delicious.

Chris' parents had a summer place here in Clayton and were opera singers. While here they taught voice and sometimes sang at the Methodist Church. Inger had visited with Chris and his parents about seven years ago and like most of us who visit, are prone to make this our home. Inger and Chris Smith hail from the Houston area and were in the food business. They decided to move to Rabun County about six

years ago with Shane, their five year old daughter.

Inger had always thought of herself as a Southerner, being from Texas, until they were invited to a party, along with Chris' parents, at the home of Ernestine and Ralph Dickerson. She noted that this kind of entertaining was indicative of Southern charm. Prior to dinner they enjoyed cocktails and becoming acquainted with the other guests. When dinner was about to be served, Ernestine rang a dinner bell. This was indeed the Southern way of entertaining.

When they returned home to Texas, this stayed in Inger's mind and they started a dinner club with six other couples, who were also in the food business. One of the rules was that a dinner bell must ring as dinner was served. It was not easy finding dinner bells in their area. Some of the members bought antique dinner bells and Chris even made one in his blacksmith shop, using this for barbeque dinners (This is truly a couple with varied talents!) The club became known as The Dinner Bell Club. At times the supper club invites other couples to join them for the evening but must be voted in by all the members of the club. Can you imagine what their dinners must be like? This provides wonderful memories of times spent here in Clayton.

Inger's has been opened for one year now and I inquired about the addition to the building. I was glad to learn that Inger does not want to enlarge her place, but wants to maintain the quality of the food and enjoy the uniqueness of her present surroundings. The reason for the addition is that Inger brings the food to the restaurant from her commercial kitchen in Lakemont. Realizing this was an imposition on her client, Claudia Taylor, landlady, opted to enlarge the kitchen where Inger could cook on the premises.

She decided to add a deck for outdoor dining. Isn't this wonderful? Inger is thinking of doing private parties in the evenings with the appropriate wine to be served along with dinner. Chris was in the wine business in Houston for five years and is most knowledgeable in this area as well.

This being the month of February when it is still cold enough to enjoy some good soup, I asked Inger to share a few of her soups with us. I might add that Inger does not use a recipe, as is the case with all good cooks and chefs. So enjoy the taste treats Inger gives us. February is the Love Month and love certainly shows in this wonderful family.

Creamy Artichoke Soup

2 lbs. Artichoke hearts, preferably fresh, but canned are okay.
Juice of one lemon
1/2 stick butter
1/2 cup white wine
6 cups vegetable or chicken stock
2 tsp. Thyme leaves
1 cup Parmesan cheese
1 cup heavy cream
salt and pepper

In a four-quart pot, sauté artichoke hearts in lemon juice, butter, white wine and salt and pepper to taste. Cook until artichokes are golden and softened. Add stock and simmer for 15 minutes. Add thyme, parmesan cheese and cream. Using an emulsion blender, puree soup. Cook for 10 more minutes and taste for seasoning. Add salt and pepper if desired.

Easy Borscht

3 Tbs. unsalted butter
2 medium onions, finely chopped
4 leeks, white part only, washed and minced
1 celery rib, diced
1 medium turnip, diced
2 cloves garlic, diced
2 lbs. peeled and trimmed beets, cut into 1/4 inch dice
5 cups beet broth
5 Tbs. white wine vinegar
Salt and pepper
Creme Fraiche or sour cream
Chopped dill
Slices of black bread

Melt butter in a four-quart pot over medium heat. Add vegetables and cook for 15-20 minutes or until they are soft. Add broth and bring soup to a simmer. Simmer slowly for 10 minutes. Make sure all veggies have softened thoroughly. Sprinkle in vinegar, season with salt and pepper to taste, serve hot. Dollop with sour cream, sprinkle dill on top. Serve with black bread - enjoy!

March, 2005

*I*t was a cold and rainy winter day as Martha and I sat in her living room over coffee and muffins warm from the oven spread with jam made from Concord eating grapes on the Ezzard farm. The weather did nothing to dampen our spirits as the scenery through this many-windowed house afforded views of the vineyard, the distant mountains, the rolling hills and the wonderful cloud formations for us to enjoy.

The house is most unusual and was designed by their artist daughter, Shelly Ezzard-Smith. One room opens to the other from the foyer, to the living room, dining room, large stairway and kitchen. A huge fireplace can be enjoyed from each room. As everyone knows, the kitchen is the heart of any home. The Ezzards chose cherry wood for their cabinets and housing for the appliances which look like furniture. Martha told me that the work was done by North Georgia craftsmen.

Winding my way up to the house, I noticed a field where bushes were planted with what looked like identifying plaques. I inquired about this and Martha told me it was their arboretum, as she is a tree-hugger. She once attended a seminar entitled, "Dancing with Trees", where she slept in a tree all night. She went on to explain that each grandchild is encouraged to plant a tree of their own choosing. They must reach the age of four, thus enabling them to remember this adventure. The trees are labeled with the name of the child planting the tree and the species of the tree, chosen by the grandchildren themselves.

As I looked around, I noticed the variety of artwork. These included art by their daughter Shelly, various Georgia artists, and photos by Peter McIntosh, which Martha particularly enjoys.

Martha went on to tell me that the making of wine begins in the vineyard in the winter. John does much of the pruning and spraying himself. He loves working on the land which has been in his family

for five generations on his mother's side of the family. John V. Arrendale had one of the early land grants. As John was growing up the land was used as a dairy and creamery. They grew the usual vegetables which were sold at a roadside stand. Many Rabun County natives have picked the delicious blueberries from this land and used the honor box. When the box disappeared last summer, the grandchildren made and painted another honor box. John has always felt the pull back to the land of his childhood even though he enjoyed a successful practice in urology in the Denver area. Martha was a practicing lawyer and served in the State Legislature. She recognized John's desire to return to the land of his ancestors and was instrumental in making the move back home which took place in 1993. She now writes part-time for the Atlanta Journal-Constitution and John practices part-time in his chosen field of Urology with Dr. Guy Gober in Tiger.

John became aware of the fact that grapes for wine-making could be grown in this part of the country. He did much research and visited vineyards in Northeast Georgia and particularly in Virginia. Martha and John nurtured and planted their first grapes in 1995 which proved to be a successful endeavor. Friends Bill and Leckie Stack owned an orchard in Tiger for many years, and in 1998

John and Bill produced an exceptional wine in a couple of barrels in Bill's basement. They decided to form a partnership and start a winery in the old creamery building which they named Tiger Mountain Vineyards. Bill was instrumental in finding and obtaining the necessary equipment and licenses required to carry out this endeavor. In the fall of 2000 they constructed a barrel room and released their first wine at a fall annual harvest.

After discussing recipes, Martha asked if I would like to see the winery and we hurried through the pouring rain to see where the wine is kept in barrels at just the right temperature. Daughter Shelly designed the labels for the wine bottles which won two awards in California. One begins to realize the research, hard work and expertise it takes to produce a good wine upon seeing these things. The Ezzard vineyard is 10 years old this year. Martha presented me with a bottle of Rabun Red, one of her favorites.

As I drove down the winding drive away from the house I stopped to appreciate the views this land provides. Imagine living on the land which has been in your family for five generations and to continue using the land in a different, imaginative and productive way. Martha told me that a variety of rose bushes have been planted at the end of each row of grapes. Can you imagine the beauty of this during the blooming season? This is another view of the land I would like to enjoy. My visit with Martha proved to be a wonderful way to spend a rainy winter day.

Shrimp Fettucine
with Tiger Mountain Viognier

1 T. butter
1 tsp. minced garlic
2 T. minced fresh parsley
1/2 lb. shrimp, peeled and deveined
2 T. Tiger Mountain Viognier
   (or other white wine)
3 T. butter
1/2 cup of heavy cream
1/4 cup freshly grated Parmesan cheese
1/4 tsp. salt
1/8 tsp. freshly ground pepper
8 oz. Fettucine, cooked al dente and drained
red pepper flakes
1 avocado, peeled, pitted and sliced

In large skillet, heat 3 T. butter until melted; add minced garlic and cook 1 minute. Add parsley, shrimp, and white wine and cook for two minutes, until shrimp turns pink. Transfer to small bowl.

In the same skillet, heat 3 T. butter. Reduce heat to low and add cream, Parmesan and red pepper flakes (a shake or two!) Cook 3 minutes until cheese melts and sauce is smooth (do not allow boil). Pour over fettucine and add sliced avocado on top.

Mushroom Roll Ups

6 T. of butter
1/2 lb. Mushrooms, finely chopped
4 T. green onion, chopped
3 T. flour
12-14 slices white bread
salt and pepper to taste

Trim crusts from bread and flatten on both sides with rolling pin. Saute onion in butter one minute. Add chopped mushrooms (may chop in food processor) Saute onions and mushrooms 2-3 minutes. Gradually add flour. Spread paste-like mixture thinly on flattened bread. Roll up tightly and cut each in half (making two roll-ups of each piece of rolled bread).

Place in freezer overnight. Prior to serving, melt 1/2 stick butter or margarine and dip each frozen roll-up. Place back in freezer. (May be done several hours ahead)

Bake in 400 degree oven 10 minutes or until brown and crusty.

2 Dozen - Excellent appetizer, red wines.

April, 2005

Across the table from

Rebekah Krivsky

As Rebekah and I chatted in her sitting room, we reminisced about old times and talked of people we knew. This is the fourth house in which I have visited Rebekah, having known Rebekah and her husband, Jerry, for many years. I remembered attending a baby shower for their first son, Lee. Three more sons followed him. It was a household where men held the majority. It must have seemed different when daughters-in-law joined the family. They now have five grandchildren. Rebekah and I belonged to a ladies bridge club as well as a couples club and I remember we produced the most delicious dinners and played bridge until all hours of the morning.

Rebekah and Jerry met on Lake Rabun in 1957 where both of their parents had homes. Rebekah's family visited here early on and rented places for a few summers then bought a home in 1953. Her family was from Camilla, Georgia, and she attended college in Virginia. Jerry's family was from Chicago and when he graduated from military school, they moved here permanently to Lake Rabun in 1956. George and Marge Krivsky started a business and planned to manufacture aluminum luggage, which did not prove to be feasible. They went into other metal stamping jobs and named their business Rabun Products, but most of us here called it the luggage factory.

When meeting in 1957, after their freshman year in college, they married in December of 1958. Rebekah transferred to the University of Georgia where Jerry was in college. He had two years remaining in his military service and after graduation they were moved to Monmouth Beach, New Jersey, and then to Ft. McClellan, Alabama. After Jerry completed his tour of duty, they moved to Rabun County where Jerry took over the management of Rabun Metal Products as his father chose semi-retirement at that time. When the building burned in 1965

they rented a building in downtown Tiger and began to make bed rails and bed frames. At the present time, they manufacture occasional tables, baker's racks, wheels for go-carts, and parts for O'Cedar Mops.

The Krivskys moved into their current home in August of last year, the home being built in 1937. This is the Claude and Rose Derrick home, one which Rebekah enjoyed visiting on many occasions since she was friends with Claudia, their daughter. This house holds happy memories for Rebekah and she grew to love it. It sits on a seven-acre hill right in the middle of Clayton and views can be enjoyed from every angle.

The house is high-ceilinged and has many windows, reflecting the architecture of the era. The dining room and living room are painted in a lovely fawn color with white trim and double crown molding. French doors lead to the living room and another set from the living room to the covered porch. The home has three full fireplaces housing gas logs, which are now so popular. The bathrooms have herringbone tile floors and there are transoms over some of the solid doors into the bedrooms. The heating system, which is a hot water system fueled by oil, stands in the middle of the house and they call this the boiler room. This will be converted to natural gas as renovations continue. Jerry has done some of the renovations himself, particularly in the bathrooms.

They enjoy many of their favorite findings from Europe, such as a chandelier from Venice and a framed fan from Spain. Rebekah is especially fond of a pastel done by her father's cousin in 1894.

Lee and Emmett continue in the business with their father, who is semi-retired. Kevin is a manufacturing representative and lives on Lake Lanier in Gainesville. Allen is an engineer living in Marietta and is part owner in a firm there. Lee is also the preacher at Antioch Methodist Church out on Warwoman. This couple has been very active in community affairs, Jerry being past president of the Rotary Club, the Jaycees, and Boy Scout Leader. All four boys made Eagle Scout, which is quite an accomplishment. Rebekah is active in the American Heart Association, Relay for Life, March of Dimes Walk for America, and is a past president of Rhapsody in Rabun. They have been members of the Methodist Church in Clayton since 1962 and now divide their time between this church and the Antioch Methodist Church.

Rebekah and I then turned to recipes, some from her family and friends in Camilla. I would love to include them all but have chosen three I know you will enjoy.

Onion Casserole
Laurie Collins, Camilla, GA

2 large Vidalia onions (2lbs.) sliced
2 T butter, melted
1 can cream of chicken soup, undiluted
1/2 cup milk
1 tsp. soy sauce
2 cups (8 oz.) shredded Swiss cheese
1/2 loaf of French bread

Sauté onions in butter and spoon into an 8x12x2" casserole. Combine soup, milk and soy sauce; pour over onions. Sprinkle cheese evenly over sauce. Cut bread into 3/4" slices; arrange on top. Brush bread with butter. Bake at 350 degrees for 30 minutes or until bread is golden brown.

Spoon Bread

1 pint sweet milk
6 T butter
1 cup cornmeal
1 tsp. Salt
3 eggs, room temperature, separated

Scald milk (do not boil); stir in butter, cornmeal and salt. Cook, stirring constantly, until cornmeal comes away from sides of pan and thickens. Set aside to cool until lukewarm. Add beaten egg yolks; mix thoroughly. Fold in stiffly beaten egg whites; mix gently but thoroughly. Poured into greased and floured 2 quart baking dish and bake at 375 degrees for 1 hour or until top is golden brown. Serve immediately. Yield: 6 servings.

Roasted Vegetables

4 medium-size red potatoes,
    cut into 8 wedges
1/4 cup olive oil
4 garlic cloves, pressed
1 tablespoon dried thyme
1 1/2 tsp. salt
1/4 tsp. pepper
1 purple onion, sliced
1 zucchini, quartered
1 yellow squash, quartered
1 portobello mushroom, quartered

Toss together first 6 ingredients in a large bowl and turn in to a 15x10 jelly roll pan. Bake in preheated 400 degree oven for 20 minutes. Add onion and next 3 ingredients, and bake, stirring occasionally, 15 more minutes.

Serves 6. Very good with pork chops and pork roast. (One of the family's favorites.)

May, 2005

L. to R.: Janie P. Taylor, Donna Findley, Myrtle Speed, Iris Patterson, Nancy Bean, Moniree Ledford, Margie Bleckley and Roma Owens

Across the table from

The Senior Quilters

The phone rang, and it was my friend Janie P. Taylor. She asked if I would like to come to the Senior Center in Tiger to meet the quilters and to talk about some of their favorite "old timey" recipes, which they carry to homecomings and family reunions. The idea immediately appealed to me. The day I visited, the ladies were working on a printed pattern.

They explained that most are hand-pieced patterns but each member chooses the quilt she would like to use in her home. They meet several times a week, chat, have lunch together and share recipes and in due time another quilt is completed. There are many patterns to choose from, the most popular being the log cabin pattern. Now let's meet the ladies:

ROMA OWENS ~ Roma was originally from the rural Eagle Lake Community in Florida, where her family engaged in vegetable truck farming. She resides in Rabun Gap with her husband, Martin, and they have four children and eight grandchildren. They attend Taylor's Chapel Baptist Church. The teacakes were made by her grandmother and were always on hand for the children and grandchildren to enjoy. Just reading the recipe brings back wonderful and happy memories of childhood and home to Roma.

Old Fashioned Teacakes

2 1/4 c. sifted plain flour
1/4 tsp. salt
2 tsp. baking powder
1/2 c. butter
1 c. sugar
2 eggs, beaten
1/2 tsp. vanilla
1 Tbsp. Milk

Sift flour, salt and baking powder together. Cream butter, sugar and eggs together. Add vanilla, milk and dry ingredients. Blend well. Place dough on a lightly floured board, sprinkle a little flour over the dough and roll to about 1/2 inch thick. Cut with cookie cutter. Place on cookie sheet and bake in a moderate oven (350ø or 375º) for about 12 to 15 minutes or until lightly browned on top.

NANCY W. BEAN ~ Nancy was raised in Whitefish Bay, Wisconsin and has resided in Rabun County since 1999. She attends the First United Methodist Church in Clayton. She has one child and two grandchildren. Her family recipe is inherited from her mother and recalls big picnics sponsored by the Shriners while growing up.

Baked Spaghetti

1 - 16 oz. box regular spaghetti (break in half and cook as directed)
1 large onion, diced
1 large (28 oz.) can and 1 small (14 1/2 oz.) can whole tomatoes
1 lb. sharp or extra sharp cheddar cheese, sliced
salt, pepper, margarine or butter

Grease 3-quart casserole. Make layers on rotation - spaghetti, margarine, sliced onion, salt and pepper, cut up tomatoes, cover with cheese. Repeat. Half way add tomato juice, and again when finished. Not too much, shouldn't be soupy. Bake at 350° for 45 minutes.

MYRTLE SPEED ~ Myrtle was raised in the Warwoman community, and has lived there all her life. She has seven children, 13 grandchildren, and 12 great grandchildren. She is a lifetime member of the Antioch Methodist Church and enjoys attending the annual Hale Ridge Homecoming on the first Sunday in September. Prior to the homecoming, the community cleans and beautifies the enclosed cemetery. The old Hale Ridge Baptist Church had been discontinued. Myrtle likes to take her favorite recipe for potato salad.

Potato Salad

3 c. cooked potatoes, sliced
2-3 Tbsp. grated onion
1 tsp. mustard
1/2 c. chopped sweet pickles
4 hard cooked eggs, chopped
Mayonnaise to moisten
Salt and pepper to taste

Mix potatoes, onion, mustard, pickles and eggs. Chill several hours. Add enough mayonnaise to moisten. Season to taste. Makes six servings.

DONNA D. FINDLEY ~ Donna is from Pennsylvania and has been living in this area for five years. She now lives in Clayton and attends the Carver's Chapel Baptist Church. This recipe is over 100 years old and comes to us from her grandmother. This was a favorite for Thanksgiving and Christmas family dinners.

Pecan Puffs

1 c. Crisco, spray, or oleo
4 Tbsp. sugar
2 tsp. vanilla
2 c. cake flour
2 c. pecans, chopped

Mix all ingredients together and roll into small balls, place on greased baking sheet and bake at 300° for 45 minutes or until done. While still hot, roll in powdered sugar then roll again when cool.

IRIS PATTERSON ~ Iris has been in Rabun County all her life, a member of the Holt family in Mountain City. She now lives in Scott's Creek Community, and is well known for her quilting. She attends the Mt. Calvary Baptist Church, and Iris shares her company yeast rolls with us.

Company Yeast Rolls

1 pkg. dry yeast
1/3 c. warm water
1 c. warm milk
1/3 c. melted butter or shortening,
    plus more for dipping rolls
1/4 c. sugar
1 tsp. salt
3 1/2 to 4 c. of flour

Dissolve yeast in warm water. Mix together warm milk, melted butter, sugar and salt. Mix together the yeast and milk mixture. Gradually stir in flour. Mix for 5 minutes. Cover the dough and let rise until doubled in bulk. Roll out dough and cut with a biscuit cutter. Dip each round into melted butter and place in a pan. Cover with a cloth and let rise for 1 1/2 hours. Bake in a 350° oven for 30 minutes. Yield: 25-30 rolls.

MARGIE BLECKLEY ~ Margie now resides in Mountain City, but her younger years were spent in the Warwoman Community. She attends the Pleasant Hill Baptist Church where her Fresh Apple Cake is a regular item at their annual homecoming each summer.

Fresh Apple Cake

2 c. sugar
1 1/2 c. oil
3 eggs
1/4 c. orange juice
1 tsp. vanilla
3 c. plain flour
1 tsp. soda
1/4 tsp. salt
1 tsp. cinnamon
1 c. chopped apples
1 c. chopped pecans
1 c. coconut

Mix sugar, oil, eggs, juice and vanilla. Sift flour, salt, soda and cinnamon. Add to first mixture. Stir in apples, coconut and pecans. Pour in greased and floured tube pan. Bake at 325° for 1 hour and 20 minutes or until cake leaves sides of pans.

Glaze
2 c. 10X sugar
1/2 c. orange juice
water (enough to make pouring consistency)

Pour over hot cake in pan. Make sure it runs down sides. Let stand 15 minutes before turning out of pan.

MONIREE LEDFORD ~ Moniree is a native mountaineer, born and raised in Clay County, North Carolina. She moved to Rabun County in 1956 with her husband, Chloe and family. They have three children. She has happy memories as a youngster of riding in the back of the pick-up to attend an all day singing with dinner on the grounds sharing with kin and friends. She attends the Battle Branch Baptist Church. Moniree shares her oatmeal cake with us.

Oatmeal Cake

Pour 1 1/2 c of boiling water over 1 cup of quick oatmeal, let stand to cool while you prepare the batter

1 c. brown sugar
1 c. white sugar
1/2 c. Wesson oil or melted Crisco
2 whole eggs

Sift together 1 1/2 cups of flour, 1 tsp. cinnamon, 1/2 tsp. soda, 1/2 tsp. salt. Add to the above ingredients, mix in oatmeal and pour into a greased and floured pan. Bake 35 to 40 minutes at 350°

Icing
1 stick margarine
1 c. brown sugar
1/2 c. evaporated milk.

Cook while constantly stirring and boil down until thick. Add vanilla and one can of coconut. Pour onto cake while both cake and icing are warm.

JANIE P. TAYLOR ~ Janie is a native of Rabun County and a retired educator. She is a descendant of the Arrendale family and lives in the Tiger area. She is a member of the Tiger United Methodist and has four children, and ten grandchildren. This bread was her mama's recipe and Mama Clyde always fixed it for the regular Rabun County Singing Convention when it met in Tiger. People from far and near joined in the day-long singing and dinner on the grounds.

Steam Boston Brown Bread
2 c. whole wheat flour
1 c. yellow cornmeal
1 tsp. baking soda
1 1/2 tsp. low-sodium baking powder
1 tsp. cinnamon
1 c. seedless raisins
1/2 c. chopped nuts (pecan or walnuts)
1/4 c. unbleached flour
2 c. buttermilk or sour milk
1/2 c. molasses

Wash carefully and dry three number 2-size cans (about 2 1/2 c. capacity). Coat the insides generously with vegetable oil or soft margarine and set aside.

In a large mixing bowl, stir together the whole wheat flour, cornmeal, baking soda, baking powder, and cinnamon. Stir in raisins, nuts, and unbleached flower. Add the buttermilk or sour milk and the molasses; stir just until all the dry ingredients are moistened.

Spoon the batter into the cans. Cover the tops with a double thickness of waxed paper and tie securely with string. Place the cans on a rack in a large kettle and add boiling water to a level within two inches of the tops of the cans. Cover the kettle tightly and steam 2 1/2 hours or until done. (Check several times during cooking period and add more water if needed.)

Lift cans from hot water, remove paper and string and place on a rack to cool for 10 minutes. Then remove the bread from the cans (use a knife to loosen around the edges, if needed) and finish cooling the loaves on the rack. Serve warm or cold, yields 8 to 10 servings (3 loaves).

I certainly enjoyed my time spent with the quilters and to see and learn more about this wonderful art form. I thank them for having me and I give special thanks to Janie for inviting me.

Marquez & Jack Martin

I had a delightful visit with Marquez and Jack Martin last week up on Payne Hill. We sat down to coffee and Key Lime Pie. I complimented Marquez on the dessert and learned later that Jack had made this. He enjoys cooking right along with Marquez in preparing for their many dinner parties. When they built their house they changed a clothes closet off the entry to shelves that would hold cookbooks and it is full. He showed me a copy of "The Joy of Cooking." How many of you remember this book?

The Martin's met through mutual friends and came to Clayton in 1955, Marquez coming from Hartwell and Jack from Williamston, South Carolina. He attended Brevard College when it was a two-year school and then transferred to the University of Georgia. Jack was a Vocational Agriculture teacher at Rabun County High School and developed their ornamental horticulture department. I remember going to the school to purchase plants for my garden.

Marquez began the first kindergarten here in Rabun County and enjoyed this for 14 years. She held graduation services each year at the Clayton Elementary School. They went on field trips, prepared a float for the Christmas parade, along with many other activities. So you can see this was a well-rounded program. She then attended business school in Clarkesville and served as secretary to Sam Letson, pastor of Clayton Baptist Church for 2 1/2 years. Dr. Hamby then asked her to be Administrative Assistant in his dental practice.

The Martins have two children. Jimmy lives in Elizabethtown, Tennessee, where he sells and repairs vacuum cleaners. Mary Ann lives out on Tallulah River with her husband, Steve Littrell and children, Jacob and Will.

Marquez retired in the late 70s and Jack in the 80s. These retirees thoroughly enjoy this life with their dinner parties and they have stayed in touch with many friends, seven of whom were Jack's close friends in college. They take turns planning trips together and have enjoyed visiting many areas.

Jack served as secretary, treasurer and president of the Lion's Club and stayed active for many years. Marquez enjoys playing bridge and at one time became interested

In entering cooking contests sponsored by the Farm Bureau Federation. One must win District first before entering a State contest and she took home first and second place in these, with the exception of the time she took a frozen Creme de Menthe dessert to Macon, Georgia in the summertime. Jack kept the cooler filled with ice and Marquez even called ahead to made sure she could place this in their freezer upon arrival. Well, this was the only time she took third place and they laugh now at the idea of taking a frozen dessert to Macon in the middle of summer. I have the recipe for this, but room does not allow for all of her goodies.

I have included their recipe for Stuffed Trout and Southern Style Hush Puppies along with an appetizer to enjoy while waiting for the dinner to be served. Talk about fresh fish - it doesn't get any better than this. Thank you again, Marquez and Jack, for a most pleasant and fun afternoon.

Southern Style Hush Puppies

1 cup self rising corn meal
1/2 cup self rising flour
1 tablespoon sugar
3/4 cup milk
1 egg
1 medium onion, coarsely chopped

Mix dry ingredients with milk. Mixture will be hick. Add onion and egg, beat. Refrigerate batter all day. Drop batter from a soup spoon into hot deep canola oil. Cook over medium heat 3-5 minutes or until golden brown. Yield: 3 dozen.

Baked Stuffed Trout

1 1/2 cup chicken broth
1 bay leaf
1/2 tsp. Tabasco, divided
1/2 cup uncooked, long grain rice
1/2 cup butter or margarine, divided
1/2 cup onion, chopped
1/4 cup celery, chopped
1 tablespoon parsley, chopped
1 whole fish (2 1/2 - 3 lbs.)
2 tablespoons lemon juice

In medium saucepan combine chicken broth, bay leaf and 1/4 teaspoon Tabasco. Bring to boil, add rice, cook according to package directions, discard bay leaf. In medium saucepan melt 1/4 cup butter, saute onions, celery and parsley until soft. Add remaining 1/4 teaspoon Tabasco, mix well. Combine vegetables and rice.

Wash fish and pat dry. Place fish in buttered baking dish. Stuff fish with rice mixture. Melt remaining 1/4 cup butter, stir in lemon juice. Spoon lemon butter over fish. Bake at 450 degrees for 25-35 minutes or until fish flakes easily with a fork. Yield: 4 servings

Smoked Oyster Dip

1 3 oz. package cream cheese, softened
2 tablespoons mayonnaise
1 tablespoon finely chopped onion
1 3 2/3 oz. can smoked oysters,
    drained and chopped
assorted crackers or chips

Combine cream cheese, mayonnaise, onion and oysters. Mix well and chill. Serve with assorted crackers or chips.

Across the table from
Betty Brooks

Betty stayed at home for a year after graduating from high school, after which she attended Toccoa Falls College. She took a business course and left to take a position at Wheaton College in Illinois where her brother was studying. She decided to return home and was employed by James Lees & Sons. This is where she met Buck Brooks and they were married in 1959. Buck's mother was a widow left with three small children and married T. J. Hamby and moved to Clayton. Some of you may know his sister, Liz Tomlin, who also lives in Clayton.

I first met Betty Brooks when my husband, Harry, was transferred here in 1958 from Philadelphia. We met Betty & Buck at Clayton Baptist Church and both men were employed by James Lees & Sons "makers of those heavenly carpets." Most of you will recognize the name Burlington Industries as they purchased the industry sometime later. Buck and Harry also cooked many breakfasts for the men's meeting at the church and barbecued outdoors, Buck being the chief chef and Harry and the others being the helpers.

Betty and her younger brother Bob were raised in Demorest and moved to Rabun Gap when their father, Robert Philip was called to teach at Rabun Gap-Nacoochee School. Many of you do not know that the school operated a Junior College from 1934 until 1945, when it became a public high school for the northern part of the county. It was then turned into a private school in 1978. They lived on campus and eventually Mr. Philip bought land on Darnell Creek where they built their home. He continued to teach for another 10 years.

Betty & Buck lived in the Jarrett's apartments while they built their home in Rabun Gap. They have always been active in church work. The lovely playground you see in front of the church was given in loving memory of Buck by Betty as he loved the little children. She is till active in the church work, belonging to the Women on Missions, she is my present Sunday School teacher and is in the Sanctuary choir, having a lovely soprano voice. Betty's mother, Sue Philip, sang with the Song Birds choir and at times Betty and her mother sang duets. Betty also volunteers in the music suite on Wednesday mornings where I help her. Her volunteer work does not end with the church as she spends each Tuesday in archive department of Rabun Gap-Nacoochee School.

An article on Betty would not be complete without mentioning her love of animals. She has four cats and a donkey named Barney who is 30 years old. He is a watch donkey, letting Betty know when strangers appear. He likes to visit folk a the flea market which backs up to Betty's pasture. The next time you visit, take a minute to speak to Barney as he loves the attention. He is also Betty's missionary donkey, having spent a summer at Camp Pinnacle where he befriended all of the girls attending the camp. They had set up a Bedouin village complete with a tent and vegetable garden. In the 22nd chapter of Numbers you will read about another donkey, so Barney carries on the work. Betty shares her favorite recipe for pork chops and others which she holds dear as they were her mother's recipes. Another delightful afternoon was afforded me as I interviewed Betty.

Pork Chops Supreme

pork chops (1" thick)
lemon slices
onion slices
brown sugar
catsup
salt

For each serving, trim excess fat from chop. Place in baking dish, add salt to taste. Top each chop with lemon slice, thin onion slice, sprinkle generously with brown sugar. Pour 1 tbsp. catsup over each chop. Cover and bake 1 hour. Uncover and bake 30 min. longer. Remove when juices have evaporated. Temperature - 350 degrees

Onions Scalloped
(Sue Philip's recipe, Betty's mother)

2 large onions
1 small green pepper
1 small pimento
2 cups bread crumbs
1/2 cup milk
1 tsp. salt
12 tsp. pepper

Peel and slice onions. Chop and parboil peppers for 5 min., drain. Place crumbs in buttered casserole, add a few pieces of pimento, onions, green pepper and remainder of pimento. Sprinkle crumbs on top. Add salt and pepper. Pour milk over all, cover and bake. Remove cover last 15 min. to brown crumbs. Time: 1 1/2 hour, Temp.: 350 degrees

(This dish was a family favorite. The recipe was found in "The Priscilla Cookbook", which Mother received as a wedding gift in 1927.)

Chocolate Pie
(Sue Philip's recipe, Betty's mother)

1 cup sugar (scant)
1/2 cup flour
6 Tbsp. cocoa
2 cups evaporated milk
2 eggs
1/2 stick butter or margarine
1 tsp. vanilla
pinch salt
1 baked pieshell

Mix flour, sugar and cocoa in top of double boiler. Gradually add milk, cook until thick. Add slightly beaten egg yolks and butter or margarine. Cook 4 minutes. Add egg whites which have been beaten with 1/2 cup sugar. Add vanilla, beat until smooth. Place in baked pie shell.

(Mother "made this up" after trying other recipes which she didn't like.)

August, 2005

Chris Reeves Hendricks and I chatted in her office, the main office of Reeves hardware Company where she holds the position of Corporate Secretary. This seems overwhelming but in her own capable fashion this petite mother and grandmother handles it all with ease. She reminded me of her grandmother, Rubye Reeves who was also a tiny, friendly, capable person. In fact, Rubye was one of the first people to welcome us to Clayton many years ago. As we came to know Rubye & Lewis more, our friendship grew. We took turns each monthly, enjoying dinner at different homes among the four couples who got together. We enjoyed visiting the Tudor style home where Lewis & Rubye lived, the home where Lewis, Jr. & Carol now live. Interestingly, Jeff, Chris' brother, and Sharon, along with their three daughters, now live in the home where he and Chris grew up which is just down the hill from the main house. It was especially fun when they would entertain out at Lake Burton and we took boat rides to enjoy the beauty of these surroundings. So in speaking with Chris we reminisced quite a lot. She especially remembers the toasted peanut butter and mayonnaise sandwiches her grandmother Rubye made for her.

Do you have fond memories of when a sandwich never tasted better in your life than when your grandmother made one for you? I remember my grandmother spreading soft butter (ours was always hard as a rock, being kept refrigerated) on a piece of white loaf bread, leaving just enough room to held by your thumb and sprinkling a little sugar on top - this was so special as you would never get this at home.

Chris is married to Robbie Hendricks. They have three children, Sonya, Katie, and Cliff. Robbie is a building contractor following in his father's footsteps. They live on Lake Burton on some of the land her grandfather Lewis acquired many years ago. Other members of the family have homes on the adjoining property. Katie is studying nutrition at Wester Carolina University which enters into Chris' meal planning. Cliff, a younger sibling, lives in the home.

Getting back to reminiscing, I belonged to a Ladies Ridge Club with Barbara and Lou. Barbara and Lou were Lewis and Rubye's oldest daughters. They had two younger siblings, Lewis Jr. and Fran. All four children have contributed time in the Reeves business. Lewis and Fran are still currently working there. I also know Chris' maternal grandmother, Della Watts from the Music and Literacy Club and her mother Carol from the Junior Woman's Club. Della is in her 90s with a very sharp mind. She has lived all her life in Tiger. Imagine all the wonderful stories she can share with her grandchildren and great grandchildren, there's a wealth of information here. I'd like to interview her someday.

As Chris and I discussed cooking, she expressed her concern for the lost art of cooking, especially when the family gathered in the kitchen to help with meal preparation. Our culture has changed due to the fact that most mothers are working mothers. Fast food and prepared meals are the order of the day in many homes as time does not permit for the leisure preparation of meals.

Today Chris gives us some easy salads that she loves to prepare. Most of the ingredients may be kept in your pantry for easy access and one can always pick up the fresh things such as tomatoes, peppers, etc. on the way home. You can be sure they are kid friendly and nutritional at the same time. Do let the children help with preparation, thus enabling them to pass along the memories and the art of cooking to their families.

Chris, thank you for the enjoyable time we spent together. In fact, I was so hungry for a salad, I stopped at the store and purchased the regular items needed to make a salad. I can't wait to try your special salads. So, make the summer more enjoyable for you and your family by enjoying Chris' recipes.

HAPPY SUMMERTIME!

Bean-Dorito Salad

2 tomatoes chopped
1/2 green pepper chopped
1/2 purple onion chopped
1 bag of Doritos
1 bottle of Catalina dressing
2-3 cans of pinto or black beans *(black beans are our favorite!)* drained & washed
2 cups grated cheese

Mix all of above except chips - stir in crushed Doritos prior to serving.

Garden Pasta Salad

3 cups rotini pasta, cooked & drained
2 cups broccoli flowerets
1/2 cup grated Parmesan cheese
1/2 cut each chopped red pepper,
    green pepper & slivered red onions
fresh mushrooms sliced (optional)
1 cup house Italian dressing
2-3 tablespoons of mayonnaise

Toss all ingredients in large bowl. Refrigerate.

Easy Noodle Salad
(Kid friendly)

1 box spaghetti noodles
frozen petite green peas
chopped ham
Italian dressing

Cook noodles as directed. Place frozen peas in bottom of colander. Pour pot of prepared noodles (including water) over peas. Rinse with cold water and drain. Add chopped ham and enough dressing to be good and moist. This last for days. You can add more dressing if dry.

o you know someone who is always Johnny on the spot?" When there is a need, they are the first to show up at the scene to help. Such a couple is Winona and Max Gates. I have known them since they moved to Rabun County in 1972 and I continue to enjoy the association.

Winona was born in Valdosta, Georgia. Her father was a teacher and moved into full-time ministry. A teacher he had hired along the way became his wife. Winona is an only child and has never regretted this. I understand as I too was an only child and enjoyed some of the advantages this afforded.

Winona graduated with a degree in Elementary Education from Mercer University in Macon. Her first teaching position was in Lake City, Fl. She met a young man who was with the U.S. Forest Service, being transferred there from Arkansas. He had a black and white hardtop Oldsmobile that Winona just loved. They met on her first day there and went out on a date the very next day. Max was dating a nurse and when she was rotated to the night shift, Winona made her move. I think Winona liked more than that black and white hardtop coupe.

Max grew up in the Little Rock area where his father was a farmer. During the depression, it was extremely difficult to raise a family. They migrated to Boise, Idaho to pick fruit, joining the Okie movement. They all piled into their car pulling behind it a 12' trailer much like a covered wagon with a rounded hoop top. All the children rode in this. This was in 1936 when Max was 8 years old. They pitched a tent and slept by the side of the road at night. Since they were only able to travel 25 mph, it took them 3 weeks to reach their destination. They ate light bread (loaf bread) and cheese all the way out. I asked Max if he still ate this and he said he does.

Upon arrival, they picked peaches, apples, cherries and apricots. Max remembers the Hispanics harmonizing with each other from tree to tree, and he fondly remembers and enjoys this music. It was always pleasant to his ear. When they received news that their grandmother had died, after being there for 3 months, they went back to Arkansas. Since times were still hard, his father decided they could cut logs for the lumber company. This was when Max decided he needed to further his education. He went to the University of Monticello in Arkansas that is now part of the University system and is known as the University of Arkansas-Monticello. He planned to major in industrial education, but one day he noticed some fellows piling into the back of a pick-up truck to go to work in the woods. Since Max loved the great outdoors, he decided right then and there that this was for him and changed his major to forestry. He loves to fish, especially for trout, and he and Winona often travel out West to catch and cook the fresh fish that night for supper - how wonderful. During his career they have been transferred to many places which afforded them the opportunity to see many parts of the country and to meet new people.

Max and Winona did not have a long courtship as they met in August and were married the next March. Before being married, Winona was fixing up their apartment in

Lake City, Fl. Max stayed in a Victorian house across the street. His parents were to arrive just a few days before the wedding and they arrived early, very early. Imagine a bride-to-be trying to ready their apartment, teaching school, attending her bridal showers, cooking and taking care of her new in-laws. This was a great test, but Winona passed with flying colors. At this time, Max was called to fight one of the largest forest fires Florida's history, which broke out near Lake City. Max's father wanted to go out and find Max and take him some food, and they had to do some tall talking to keep him from doing this. The Forest Service did let Max off to be married the Friday before Easter. Winona's father performed the ceremony in Greenville, Fl.

Max and Winona have two children. Steve lives in Satolah with his wife Judy and their three boys. Julie, who is an R.N., lives in Evans, Georgia, right outside of Augusta with her husband Fred and three children.

The Gates moved to Rabun County in 1976, moving from Walhalla, S.C. where she taught school and led the choir. Upon moving here, Winona took extended courses in order to teach music at Tiger Elementary School. She was pianist for 20 years and at times Choir Director at Clayton Baptist Church. I played the organ for some of this time and we enjoyed playing duets. She retired in 1996 and enjoys volunteering at the MAC (Ministry & Activities Center at CBC). Max retired from the Forest Service in 1986 and is now with Century 21 Poss Realty.

Even after knowing this couple for all these years, the story of Max migrating with the Okies was new to me and I thought it fascinating. We enjoyed coffee and Winona's coconut custard pie with our coffee. We reminisced about old times and talked about current times. Thank you, Winona and Max, for a very enjoyable evening. Now to Winona's recipes she shares with us:

Chicken Casserole

Mix together
 2 c. cooked, chopped chicken,
 2 c. chicken broth,
 1 can cream of chicken soup.
 Pour into casserole baking dish (sprayed with Pam).

Mix together thoroughly
 1 stick melted Oleo,
 1 c. flour,
 1 c milk.
 Pour over chicken, punching holes in the mixture to allow it to drizzle into it. Bake at 350 degrees until browned and bubbling - (about 45 min.)

Glorified Macaroni

1 8 oz. box elbow macaroni, cooked & drained (at times I use more).
1 lb. shredded cheese,
1 can cream of mushroom soup,
1 c. mayonnaise,
1/2 c. chopped bell pepper,
1/2 c. diced pimento.

 Mix all ingredients together and pour into a large casserole dish. I spray dish with Pam. Top with saltine cracker crumbs and dot with liquid Oleo (or dot with Oleo). Bake at 350 degrees for 30-40 minutes until bubbly. 1/2 c. chopped onion may be added to ingredients if desired.

Coconut Custard Pie

Combine 3 beaten eggs,
1 1/2 c. sugar,
1/2 c. melted Oleo,
4 tsp. lemon juice,
1 tsp. vanilla,
1 1/3 c. flaked coconut.

 Pour into an unbaked pie shell in 9" pie pan. Bake at 325 to 350 degrees about 40 min. until firm in center. Cool before serving. Delicious when served with a scoop of ice cream.

October, 2005

Across the table from

Karen Jarrell

Karen and I sat in her dining area and chatted while enjoying farm cheese and crackers. The room was newly painted in a wonderful taupe color with a lighter complimentary color on the top which will be divided by a chair rail. She and Robin plan to install crown molding around the top of the room. The dining area sat in a large bay window, an island stood in the center of the room in front of glass doors which opened up to the deck. The room continued with the kitchen appliances, a very lovely space. I would love to see it when it is completed.

Some of you may recognize Karen Jarrell as Karen Croom. Her mother and father were teachers here in Rabun County. Venita taught music, then was librarian and Clayton was a teacher of the sciences. Karen showed me a book of poems her dad had written about some of the students he taught each year. There was one poem to our son, Steve, who chose Clayton as his Star Teacher. I enjoyed reading through the poems which brought back memories of by-gone days.

Karen and Robin met through a mutual friend when she went to her first teaching assignment in Habersham County. Robin was with N. E. Georgia Technical School and is now employed at National Textiles here in Rabun County. Karen followed in her mother's footsteps as librarian in the schools which is now entitled Media Specialist.

Karen moved to Rabun County and built a home on Seed Tick Road. She and Robin married in 1984 and lived there for five years before building their own home in the Tiger community. They have a daughter, Kayla, who is a senior at Rabun County High School and is a cheerleader. She plans to further her education in the field of Sonography. In this age of technology, this is a wise choice and she and her parents are looking into the different schools where Kayla can complete her education.

Karen's hobbies include golf, tennis, walking daily and biking. She and her dad biked with a group from the Clayton Baptist Church to New Smyrna Beach. They got as far as Flagler Beach when the wind blew so strongly that if they turned around, all they had to do was steer - but this was in the wrong direction. Therefore, the trucks picked them up and took them to their final destination. This was quite an endeavor and they still enjoy riding their bikes together.

Robin and Kayla enjoy riding four-wheelers on safe trails. They have found these trails in the Toccoa area, thus affording a safe hobby.

All of them participate in activities at Clayton Baptist Church. Karen taught Sunday school for 25 years, is a member of the Bell Choir and is active in "See you at the Pole" which is held at the high school. She plays a big part in youth activities and helps with the baptism that CBC holds each year at the home of Mary Anne and Steve Littrell out on Coleman River. After the baptism, there is a cook-out following in the true Baptist tradition.

Robin is active in Sunday School and after the game fellowship at the Multi Activity Center (the MAC) at Clayton Baptist Church for the youth.

What family would be complete without pets? There is a chihuaha named Topper, a kitty name Grady and a rabbit named - what else - Thumper.

When Karen retires she would like to look into doing medical transcription from her home. She had experience in this at Ridgecrest Hospital many years ago and found that she enjoyed it.

Now Karen gives us three of her favorite recipes. She loves to cook and it was hard for her to choose - they all look so good. The Mexican Pie comes to us from Kayla which I think is neat and one she and her friends can whip up while they gather to watch a video, study or just plan to sit around and talk, which they love to do - and just think - that way you have access to your phone.

Zesty Fried Chicken

2 tablespoons cornmeal
1 teaspoon paprika
1/2 teaspoon salt
1/2 teaspoon garlic powder (optional)
1/2 teaspoon pepper
1/4 teaspoon cumin
olive oil
boneless chicken breast pieces (package)

Coat chicken breasts with cornmeal, paprika, salt, garlic powder, pepper and cumin. Heat olive oil in cooking pan on stove, add chicken breast pieces. Cook until chicken is no longer pink inside, remove from pan and enjoy.

Broccoli Casserole

1 10-oz. frozen broccoli
1 egg
1 can cream of mushroom soup
1/2 cup mayonnaise
1/2 medium onion grated
1/2 c. grated cheddar cheese
1 bag Pepperidge Farm herb stuffing mix
1/2 to 1 cup stick butter or margarine

Preheat oven to 350 degrees. Cook broccoli as directed on package. In large bowl, beat egg, add mushroom soup, mayonnaise, onion and cheddar cheese. Add broccoli and mix together well.

Pour mixture into casserole dish. Melt butter or margarine in pan (enough to make stuffing soft). mix butter/margarine with stuffing mix and sprinkle over casserole. Bake at 350 degrees for 45 minutes.

Earthquake Cake

1 1/2 cups chopped pecans
1 1/2 cups coconut
German Chocolate cake mix and ingredients to make cake
1 stick margarine
8 oz. cream cheese
4 cups powdered sugar

Preheat oven to 350 degrees. Mix chopped pecans and coconut and spread in dish. Mix German Chocolate cake mix as directed on box. Pour over the pecan-coconut mixture. Melt margarine and cream cheese in microwave. Blend with powdered sugar. Bake about 45 minutes. Test with a knife and if still gooey, bake about 5 more minutes. Don't overbake!!

Pat Marcellino and I sat over coffee at The Cottage Door. It is always pleasant to chat with Don & Sylvia Bua, proprietors, and to share a greeting with many who come in for their kick-start for the day with their favorite cup of coffee.

Before coming to Clayton, Pat and his brother had a restaurant in Del Ray Beach, FL. He brought his expertise with him when he opened a restaurant, naming it the Chick'n Coop. It was built to look like a chicken coop with windows along the top of the building. He began small and had seating for 30 people. One of the main drawing cards was his delicious Corn Fritters. When the business grew, he had the capacity to seat 350 people.

Pat is father of four children. Many of you will recognize the name of Patrick Marcellino who is a landscape architect. It is a pleasure to view the designs of this talented young man. Pat's daughter, Carolyn Ann, teaches school in Rabun County with the Head Start program. Christy teaches school in White County and Gianna lives in Atlanta. She has her own business in which she supplies temporary employment for the food service industry.

Pat's father was born in Italy and his mother in upstate New York. Pat was born in Amsterdam, N.Y., thus his N.Y. accent. I guess we never completely lose the accent of our early years. Folks recognize the fact that I still have my Philly accent. I am always disappointed as I consider myself a Southerner, having lived in the South for 40+ years. However - I am here now and I am thankful for this.

Pat likes to travel and spent five weeks recently touring Europe and spending time in Italy. He walked the streets his ancestors walked - how interesting and rewarding. Pat is very civic- oriented, being a volunteer fireman, building homes with Habitat for Humanity, working with Relay for Life and in January of this year he was elected to the Board of Commissioners here in Rabun County. Pat likes hunting, fishing and boating, so living on Lake Burton is the perfect place for him to reside. He has renovated a cabin he has had for many years.

As one would guess, Pat loves to cook and his kitchen reflects this. It measures 18x24 feet and his pride and joy is his commercial gas range. As is the custom in entertaining these days, friends and family like to gather in the kitchen and be part of the food preparation. This kitchen certainly affords plenty of room for all. I enjoyed interviewing Pat and learning more about this gentleman whom I have known these many years. He shares two of his recipes today. I knew better than to ask for a third, the famous Corn Fritter recipe.

Italian Pizzelles

Recipes from the old world. Italian Pizzelles - Thin, Crisp, Delicious. This cookie is wafer thin and has to be cooked on a special electric iron that is like a waffle iron. I like to make these at Christmas time for the family and they also make good Christmas gifts. When I was a little boy, my mother and grandmother did not have electric irons. I can remember watching them and they had cast hand irons and would put them on an open flame on top of the gas stove and also a wood stove. When it got hot they would pour the batter on the irons and close the lid and cookies would bake. After the cookies have been baked, you can sprinkle powdered sugar over them and they make a good treat with coffee or liquor.

Italian Pizzelles - 3 eggs; 1/2 teaspoon anise seed or extract (optional). I like to use anisette liquor; it gives it a better taste. Amount is up to you. 2 teaspoons baking powder; 1 teaspoon vanilla extract; 1 & 3/4 cups flour (all purpose); 1/2 cup butter, margarine or oil (melted, 1/4 lb.); 3/4 cup sugar. Beat eggs and sugar; add cooled melted butter or margarine, and vanilla and anise. Sift flour and baking powder and add to egg mixture. Batter will be stiff enough to be dropped by spoon. Batter can be refrigerated to be used later. Makes 30 pizzelles.

Lasagna

To start the making of lasagna, first have a frying pan on the stove. Obtain one pound ground beef or Italian sausage; break it up and add salt and pepper to taste. Cook the meat till it is brown. When done, remove from burner and let it sit on stove. Also, obtain from store ricotta cheese, which comes in 1 and 3 lb. containers. Put ricotta cheese in the bowl; add 3-6 eggs, depending on amount of cheese. Also add some grated Parmesan cheese, chopped fresh parsley, oregano, garlic salt, black pepper, and a little sugar. After meat has cooled, add this to the mixture and stir all together. Mixture will be thick, add enough milk to mixture to make it thin enough to spread. While you are doing this, have a pot of water on stove to get hot, adding a little cooking oil. When water begins to boil, add lasagna noodles. They come in one lb. packages. Buy as many as you see fit for your meal. Some people like to use noodles that are already cooked. I like to use regular noodles and cook them. Cook the noodles till they are almost done; take from stove and pour out hot water; let cool a little. Have some type of baking dish ready, line bottom of dish or pan with noodles. On top spread meat mixture. Do not make it thick, for you will run out of the mixture. Do this all the way to the top of dish. Some people like to mix sauce with the mixture. When you get to the top of dish and have finished arranging noodles on top of the last layer, put slices of provolone cheese. After this, put sauce on top of cheese, cover with foil and bake for around 30 to 45 minutes. Serve with garlic bread and a good salad. Mangia!!! (Eat for good health)

Across the table from
The Callahans

Today I am at the home of Bob and Marilyn Callahan. Bob is of Irish, Norwegian and Scandinavian lineage. He was born in Brooklyn, New York, and was raised Catholic when his father remarried a woman of the Catholic faith. Bob's mother died when he was six years old. He attended Catholic schools and graduated from Georgetown University. He started his career in the government arena, then went with the National Beverage Association and moved on to be Deputy General Counsel and Vice President with Coca Cola for over 20 years. He retired in 1996 and serves as President of the Lake Seed Association.

Marilyn was raised in Evansville, Indiana, and then her family moved to Miami. She attended Florida State University. She was always interested in music, being encouraged by her mother, Mary Michel, who also lived here in Rabun County. She played the ukulele and violin in the school orchestra. Marilyn began singing in high school and studied voice under Dr. Arturo di Fillipi and sang the role of Musetta with the Metropolitan Opera Stars. She also enjoyed singing in hotels, etc. When Marilyn first moved to Clayton she was soloist at the Clayton Baptist Church. I was organist at that time, so we became acquainted early on. While in Florida, Marilyn was a successful realtor, having her own agency and was a member of the Million Dollar Club. Upon moving to Clayton in 1976 she was associated with Century 21, Poss Realty. Her hobbies include Bridge, Mahjong, quilting and travel. She and Bob are both avid readers. They were preparing to leave on a cruise the following day and I thought it was very considerate of her to take time out for our interview. Bob and Marilyn married in 2001 after meeting through a mutual friend.

As one would guess, Marilyn loves to cook and was introduced to the fine art of cooking by a friend who attended the Cordon Bleu Cooking School in France. Marilyn then took cooking classes in Miami. Interestingly, her friend had two stoves, one gas and one electric. Most serious cooks prefer to cook with gas, Marilyn's choice in her home today. It has an interesting feature on it - when one turns the stove off, there is a setting for simmer which turns on and off automatically, thus avoiding the stirring and sticking process that happens frequently while making sauces.

Traditions: Bob and Marilyn entertain his family a few weeks before Christmas at Kingwood where they gather together to enjoy food, fellowship and even a band. Often the children like to entertain by singing & dancing. They exchange presents at this time thus affording the little ones to be in their own home to see what Santa brought on Christmas morning. Together Marilyn and Bob have 10 children, 24 grandchildren with one on the way and four great grandchildren, including Marilyn's family. Marilyn and Bob travel to Ponte Vedra to celebrate Christmas with her family.

Continuing the love of traditions, Marilyn always serves pork chops and spare ribs on Christmas Eve. This is accompanied by sauer kraut, applesauce and mashed potatoes. Dessert is either Mince pie or Key Lime pie. Marilyn adds apples, carroway seeds, water and sugar after rinsing her sauer kraut. On New Year's Day they celebrate with a champagne brunch consisting of ham, sweet potatoes with marshmallows, pole beans with fatback, black-eyed peas for good luck and hog jowl. (She adds tomato sauce to her green beans, onion and green pepper), homemade biscuits and ambrosia, for the Gods.

Marilyn showed me a long table with dropped leaves. This was an Irish antique Wake table over 100 years old. The body was placed on the table for viewing, then placed in a coffin and taken to the church for a later service. In the meantime the table was opened and dressed with a tablecloth and laden with food to enjoy while visiting. I thought this was a most interesting custom.

Volunteer work: Marilyn was on the first Board of Rabun Rhapsody, is active in the United Way, served for two years as President of the Music and Literary Club, is active in the Mountain Ivy Garden Club, is in the Auxiliary of Mountain Lakes Medical Center and St. Helena Alter Society.

Sauerbraten

3 lb. Beef rump roast or round
2 c. white vinegar
2 c. water
3 bay leaves
12 cloves
1 large onion thinly sliced
1 tsp. Peppercorns
1 tsp. Caraway seeds
1/4 c sugar
garlic
salt
pepper
2 Tbs. flour
1/2 c red wine
1 c sour cream
raisins

3-4 days before: Salt and pepper meat and rub with minced garlic. Heat vinegar, water and spices to just before boiling. Pour over meat in glass dish. Refrigerate covered 3-4 days, turning every day and basting.

Cooking: Wipe meat dry & strain marinade. Melt butter in heavy pan, Brown meat all sides & cover. Bake at 350 degrees for 3 hours, basting frequently. Remove meat, slice. Blend juices, flour, wine. Cook till smooth. Stir in sour cream - add raisins.

Vegetable-Relish Mold
(Serves 12)
(New Perfection Salad)

2 envelopes gelatin
1/2 cup cold water
2 cups cold water
1 1/4 teasp. Salt
1/3 cup granulated sugar
1/4 cup vinegar
1/4 cup lemon juice
2/3 cup pickle relish
1 1/2 cups shredded green cabbage
3/4 cup diced celery
3/4 cup chopped carrots
1/4 cup chopped green pepper
2 tablesp. Pimiento

Soften gelatin in cold water, add hot water and stir until dissolved. Stir in sugar and salt, vinegar and lemon juice. Cool. Add other ingredients. Mix well. Pour into 1 1/4 qt. Mold. Chill until firm. Serve with mayonnaise or French dressing.

Chicken Tettrazini

1 Green Pepper, 1 Onion, 1 c celery
(Chop & saute in butter until soft)
1 2 1/2 lb. Fryer
1 8 oz. spaghetti - Linguine
1 large can mushrooms
1 can mushroom soup
1 pack blanched almonds

Boil chicken and cook spaghetti in broth. Grease casserole. Pull chicken off bone and chop into small pieces. Layer spaghetti or linguine, chicken & sauce, repeat. Grated cheese on top. Bake at 350 degrees for 30 minutes.

Fresh Apple Pound Cake
From Robin Welch

1 1/4 cup cooking oil
1 teaspoon baking soda
2 cup sugar
3/4 teaspoon cinnamon
3 eggs
1 teaspoon salt
2 teaspoon vanilla
1 cup chopped pecans
3 cup cake flour
3 med apples peeled & diced

Combine oil, sugar and eggs. Beat at medium speed for 3 minutes then add vanilla. Combine dry ingredients (flour, soda, salt and cinnamon) and add to above mixture a little at a time. Fold in chopped pecans and apples. Put in greased and floured tube pan. Preheat oven at 325 degree. Bake for 1 hour and 20 minutes or until done.

Icing for Cake:

1 stick of butter
1 cup packed brown sugar
1/4 cup milk

Bring ingredients to a boil. Boil for 2-3 minutes. Stir for about a minute (off stove) then pour over cake. Before pouring over cake poke wholes in cake for icing to go into cake.

Breakfast Sausage Wheels
From Robin Welch

1 pd sausage
2/3 cup milk (to a full cup)
4 cup plain flour
1 teaspoon salt
1/4 cup cornmeal
2 teaspoon baking powder
1/4 cup sugar
2/3 cup oil

Mix flour, meal, sugar, salt & baking powder. Then add milk & oil., After mixing press out onto wax paper flat. Then press sausage over dough. Then carefully roll into a log. Place in freezer to get cold enough to cut into slices. (You can freeze after cutting into slices to use later). Place into a preheated oven 350 degrees for 15 - 20 minutes until done.

Breakfast Casserole
From Robin Welch

1 pkg crescent rolls
1 lb. sausage
4 eggs
3/4 cup milk
2 cups grated cheese

Press crescent rolls into rectangular baking dish. Cook sausage, drain & crumble over rolls. Mix eggs, milk and cheese. Pour over sausage. Bake at 400 degree for 20 min.

Spinach Casserole
From Dianne VanderHorst

1 lb. hamburger - brown & drain
Add 1 small chopped onion and a
little garlic powder. Cook until
onion is transparent
Add
4 oz can mushrooms,
salt & pepper
1 pkg. frozen chopped spinach (thawed),
1/2 tsp. oregano (optional)
1 can mushroom soup
1/2 cup minute rice
1 cup sour cream

Combine well and put in 8x8" pan. Top with 1/2 lb. Monterey Jack cheese Bake at 350 degrees for 30 minutes.

Bacon Roasted Pecan Poem
From Our Poetic Photographer
Peter McIntosh

Just do what I say,
'cause this ain't no jive.
Preheat the oven,
to two-seventy-five.
Some don't do it,
but I think you oughter.
You take a pound of pecans,
and soak them in water.
Drain after ten minutes,
the water'll be brown.
And in your pecans,
there'll be no bitterness found.
For treat like this,
there's just no fakin'
The flavor you get,
from a full pound of bacon.
Cut the strips into quarters,
And place them on top.
You're almost done now,
It's no time to stop.
Then four tablespoons of butter,
do add if you please,
To the 9 x 13 baking pan,
that there's no need to grease.
Add two tablespoons of sugar,
and salt just a wisp.
Keep stirring occasionally,
until the bacon is crisp.
Then drain on a towel,
until they are cool.
Congratulations my friend,
you're a pecan roasting fool.
After you cook them you can add more
sugar and salt to taste. And maybe just a
touch of Cayenne Pepper.
Place the baking pan on a sheet pan to
keep the bottom from getting too hot.

January, 2006

Across the table from

Wanda & Ed Rogers

We sat around the table enjoying Pear Pie with our coffee and then we were serenaded--yes, that's right--serenaded. This afternoon I am visiting with Wanda & Ed Rogers. Wanda was born in Greenbrier, Arkansas, and then her family moved to Benton Harbor, Michigan. She was the third in a family of eight. Ed was born in Hornersville, Missouri, which is the Boothill of Missouri, and was the last of ten children. Then his family also moved to Benton Harbor.

Wanda is a dreamer and always dreamed of meeting someone named Eddie, who would be from Texas, who would play the guitar and serenade her. This sounds like a tall order, doesn't it? But some times, the truth is stranger than fiction.

One evening Wanda and some friends were riding around the town. We have all been there. A car full of boys pulled up alongside them and suggested that they all meet at the Pizza Hut. This is how Wanda met Eddie. He had just returned from Texas and could play the guitar. Do you think this was fate? I think so. They began dating and were married two years later. The day of the wedding they awoke to a very heavy snowstorm. Ed's father had the church parking lot plowed and Ed says his Dad meant to marry him off, for sure.

Eddie became interested in the guitar when he was ten years old. His brother had won a lovely guitar in a game. Ed didn't ask any questions; he was just glad to be able to pick this instrument up when his brother wasn't around. Ed taught

recreational guitar for many years, played in a dance band and entertained at private parties. He also had a guitar shop in their basement and, of course, serenaded Wanda down through the years. So when Wanda asked him to serenade us today, he graciously complied. He is quite an accomplished musician.

Wanda was with the Department of Social Services for the State of Michigan and also with the public school system. Ed worked as a postal carrier and had a walking route. He always carried goodies for the dogs he would meet on his route. They both retired in 1991 and shortly after this they were involved in quite a serious accident. While they were recovering, they had plenty of time to talk about where they would like to spend their retirement years. Since they had visited a daughter in Atlanta on many occasions, they would take side trips up to the mountains. Their choice was to move to Clayton and they have enjoyed being here for ten years at this time and know they have made the right decision. It might be well to add here that their family consists of two children, three grandchildren and one great grandchild who are all musically inclined.

Wanda loves to cook, is a member of the Sanctuary Choir at the Clayton Baptist church and Songbird Choir, is an avid reader and does volunteer work at Clayton Baptist Church. She is also a member of the Auxilliary at Mountain Lakes Medical Center and works in the gift shop two half-days a month.

I thank you, Wanda and Ed, for a most enjoyable afternoon.

Barbeque Meatballs

3 lbs. ground beef
(I use ground round)
2 tsp. chili powder
1/2 tsp. garlic powder
2 eggs
2 C. oatmeal
1 med. onion
1 lg. can evaporated milk

Sauce
32 oz. Catsup (4 C.)
4 tbsp. Liquid smoke
1 tsp. garlic salt
2 cups brown sugar
2 tbsp. Onion flakes

Combine meatball mixture and form into balls. Combine sauce mixture and pour over meatballs. Bake at 350 degrees for 1 hour. This makes approximately 50 meatballs. Takes 2 (9X13 inch) pans, then divide the sauce between the two. To take for dinners, bake them, then put them in the crockpot to reheat or keep warm.

Wanda's Layered Lettuce Salad

1 head lettuce
3 stalks celery
1 med. Onion, chopped
1 med. Green pepper
1 pkg. Frozen green peas, cooked, drained and cooled
1 can of water chestnuts
1 T. sugar
3 to 4 oz. Parmesan cheese
BAC-O Bacon bits.

Break lettuce into bite size pieces. Save back a small portion. Alternate the above ingredients. Place the saved back portion of lettuce on top covering all. Cover all of this with 16 oz. Hellmann's low fat mayonnaise. Cover with foil and refrigerate 24 hours. (Can leave up to two days). Before serving, sprinkle with BAC-O's or bacon bits.

Pear Pie

6 cups sliced peeled ripe pears (6 pears)
1 tbsp. Lemon juice
1/2 cup plus 3 tbsp. Sugar
2 tbsp. quick-cooking tapioca
3/4 tsp. cinnamon
1/4 tsp. salt
1/4 tsp. nutmeg
1 unbaked pastry shell (9")
3/4 cup old fashioned oats
1 tbsp. flour
1/4 C. cold butter
18 caramels
5 tbsp. milk
1/4 C. chopped pecans

In a lg. bowl, combine pears and lemon juice. In another bowl, combine 1/2 C. sugar, tapioca, cinnamon and nutmeg. Add the pears, stir gently, let stand for 15 min. Pour in pastry shell. In a bowl combine the oats, flour and remaining sugar. Cut in butter until crumbly. Sprinkle over pears. Bake at 400 degrees for 45 min. In a saucepan over medium heat, melt caramels with milk. Stir until smooth, add pecans. Drizzle over pie and bake 8 ' 10 min. longer until crust is brown. Cool.

February, 2006

Jean Emhart

Shares her recipes!

Friends from out of town call - they are four hours away and would like to stop by to see you. Of course you want to reunite and welcome them to your home. You think - Oh, I would love to ask them to stay for dinner, but what on earth would I serve? We could go out to a restaurant, but I'd rather entertain here. Well, I'd like to share my easy entertaining dinner I prepared for two friends a few weeks ago.

I wanted something different, but something easy. So I went to the grocery store with no idea of what I was looking for. I browsed by the meat counter and something caught my eye. It was a small pork roast by Hormel, already flavored with onion and garlic and weighing 1 1/2 lbs.

So I decided to try it. Further down the meat counter I discovered mashed sweet potatoes by Country Crock. They were in the same type tub their butter comes in. Now I needed a relish dish and thought I'd take a can of whole cranberries and mix with a drained can of Mandarin oranges. I completed the menu with crunchy bread browned in the oven and a package of frozen mixed veggies.

PORK ROAST: The suggested cooking time was 1 hour at 325 degrees. I cooked mine for 1 1/2 hours to be sure it was done. If you have a meat thermometer, you can be sure of doneness and I plan to get one. I placed the roast in a small pan and lined it with aluminum foil, thus affording easy clean-up. The roast served three, two the day after this and I even had a plate left over for the next day. There is absolutely no waste.

SWEET POTATOES: These had an incredible flavor and took only four minutes in the microwave. The MIXED VEGGIES were also microwavable and the BREAD was browned in the oven - the kind that crumbles as you break it, so good. I placed the CRANBERRY RELISH in a pretty dish. A friend brought homemade gingerbread Christmas cookies, so this was our dessert, along with hot tea.

Since the dinner was so easy, I took extra time with my table setting. I placed a gold runner across the table, set with my Christmas dishes on gold place mats and added red goblets. I added a few candles and had soft music playing in the background.

This afforded a very festive evening without any fuss. So, the next time you need something in a hurry without giving up quality, try this easy, no fuss, no muss dinner and go ahead and enjoy your friends. You will be able to enjoy them so much more as you didn't spend hours preparing dinner before arrival.

I would like to share two of my favorite recipes with you that I enjoy. I just finished another book by Fannie Flagg. It is an easy read and so charming. If you haven't read any of her books, add her to your list. She includes recipes she uses as the story unfolds.

I took this to Thanksgiving dinner at the home of a friend. It makes a nice presentation and serves many people. I usually cut it into squares in the pan, making serving easier.

CORN CASSEROLE

1 large can cream-style corn
1 can white niblet corn
2 eggs beaten
1 stick butter
1 8 1/2 ounce box Jiffy corn muffin mix
8 ounces sour cream

Mix all ingredients together well. Put in 9X13 inch buttered dish and bake at 350 degrees for about 45 minutes, or until firm in the middle.

The next recipe is my stand-by and almost all of the ingredients may be kept in your cupboard. So, here's to easy entertaining and meals you can be proud to serve.

BEEF STROGANOFF WITHOUT PANIC

1 1/4 lb. ground beef
2 - 3 tbsp. bacon drippings
1 pkg. dry onion soup mix
Salt to taste
1/2 tsp. ginger
3 c. medium wide noodles
1 (3 oz.) can sliced mushrooms
3 1/3 c. hot water
1 c. sour cream
2 tbsp. flour

Sear ground beef in fat in saucepan. Sprinkle over beef, the onion soup mix, salt and ginger; DO NOT STIR. Arrange noodles in layers over meat; add mushrooms with liquid. Pour water over noodles, being sure all noodles are moistened. DO NOT STIR. Cover with tight fitting lid. Cook 20 - 30 minutes. Remove from heat; add sour cream mixed with flour. Stir mixture thoroughly; cook 3 - 4 minutes, serve piping hot. Yield: 6 - 8 servings. I serve with frozen peas and bread.

"Every house where love abides
And friendship is a guest,
Is surely home, and home, sweet home
For there the heart can rest."
by -Henry Van Dyke

March, 2006

Across the table from

Frances McPeak

It is my pleasure today to sit and chat with Frances McPeak. Frances is another friend I have known these many years. I also knew her mother and father with so many happy memories attached, that I knew it would be fun - and it was.

Frances was the daughter of Roy and Opal Hodgson, do the names seem familiar? Mr. Hodgson coached and taught school in several counties in Georgia and retired from the Rabun County School system. He continued his part-time work as a pharmacist at Clayton Drug which is now Clayton Pharmacy. (He had become a pharmacist before his teaching career.) He was always so friendly it always made one feel better while waiting for a prescription to be filled. Opal was nutritionist at Rabun County High School and was a fantastic cook. I have been fortunate enough to enjoy many of the meals she prepared. She was also talented as a seamstress, even making wedding dresses for some girls in the area. Opal was a member of the Sanctuary Choir at the Clayton Baptist Church, as was I. We sang the alto part and became real buddies. At times I am sure the director felt we were acting like two kids misbehaving in the classroom. I remember one time especially during a cantata that Opal had to sit down to control her laughter. I don't know how I kept it together, but I did. So indeed I have many fond memories of Frances' family. She also has a sister, Doris Edwards, who also lives in the Clayton area.

Frances had three children, Cheryl, Rodney and John Herndon. Later on Frances was employed by Georgia Power and met a co-worker named John McPeak. This union was special to me as I played the organ at their wedding at Clayton Baptist Church.

Frances enjoys many hobbies including following in her mother's footsteps by singing in the Sanctuary Choir and now she is my buddy. She served with the Red Cross as a volunteer coordinator for the Rabun County Chapter. She attends Sunday School and is a member of the Missionary Circle and Second Milers, a senior group who enjoy luncheons, speakers, shopping trips and tours together. She wants to learn how to sew and I am sure this will not be too hard with her background.

Much of her time is spent taking care of her newly acquired Cocker Spaniel, Lacey. Lacey has learned to open all of the cabinet doors and loves to get into them and make a mess, especially when Frances leaves her alone. We have all been there, I am sure. One day she got into the garbage can and it was such fun. She spread the coffee grounds, papers and all of the cans over the kitchen floor. She then proceeded to another cabinet and learned how to open Frances' Tupperware containers. Coffee must appeal to this dog as she got into freshly ground coffee and added this to the rest of the contents spread about the floor along with a dry soup mix that Frances keeps on hand. Her treat was a bag of chocolate morsels which she enjoyed with no ill effects. All of our pets afford us so much pleasure, how can we stay angry very long? Perhaps Lacey thinks that Frances had better not leave her alone anymore.

Now to the recipes Frances has provided us, some of which are her mothers, how wonderful. Thank you again, Frances for affording me a happy and rewarding interview.

Brunswick Stew (Mother's recipe)

3 lb. Chicken, cooked & deboned
3 lb. Beef, cooked & defatted
3 lb. Pork, cooked & deboned
3 - 1 lb. Cans of corn
3 - 1 lb. Cans of tomatoes
1 large onion
1 stick butter or margarine

After cooking meat, put it through a food chopper with the onion, tomatoes and corn. Add the margarine or butter and simmer 45 min. Add salt and pepper. May add tabasco, worcestershire or other seasonings as desired.

Butterscotch Bars

2 1/4 cups plain flour
2 1/4 tsp. Baking powder
1/2 tsp. Salt
1 cup butter or margarine
1 lb. Brown sugar, sifted
1 1/2 tsp. Vanilla
2 large eggs
1/2 cup water

Stir flour, baking powder and salt. Cream together the butter and brown sugar. Add vanilla, beat in eggs, one at a time. Add flour mixture and water. Beat gently until well blended. Stir in nuts. Put into well buttered 13x9x2 inch pan. Bake in a preheated oven until cake tester comes out clean in center. Cool and cut into small bars.

Oven Chicken

1 - 8 1/2 oz can crushed pineapple, lightly drained
1/4 cup vegetable oil
1/4 cup lemon juice
1/2 tsp. Lemon flavoring
1/4 cup white corn syrup
2 tbsp. Soy sauce
1 tsp. Accent
1 tsp. Salt
1/4 tsp. Ginger
1 3 lb. Chicken, cut up in pieces

Place chicken in a shallow baking dish. Combine all other ingredients and pour over chicken pieces. Bake at 375 degrees, basting frequently and turning pieces once. Bake 45 minutes to 1 hour. Place pan briefly under broiler for browning when chicken is tender.

Baked Rice

1 stick butter
1 medium onion
2 cans beef consomme
1 cup uncooked rice
1 can mushrooms (if desired)

Saute onion in butter. Combine all other ingredients and pour all into a large casserole. Cover and bake at 350 degrees for one hour.

April, 2006

Across the table from *The Gober Family*

*D*inner for eight - for most of us that would mean inviting someone to join us, but not so in the Gober household. Dr. Guy Gober and Susan have six children - Camren, Redding, Leah, Georgia, Moranel and little Guy. Susan has a lot of help in preparing meals as the children enjoy taking part in this. They built their own raised-vegetable and herb gardens along with Susan. She became interested in growing herbs and their use about 15 years ago. The children help in other ways: chopping wood, and taking care of the horses, among other things. Susan was also interested in photography and many of her photos appeared in a local newspaper.

Since Dr. Gober was born and raised in Atlanta he grew fond of the North Georgia Mountains since he is an avid cyclist. He graduated from Georgia Tech and his spring break in 1970 he spent mountain biking in these mountains. While cycling he wore a red shirt and printed on the back of it was "cycling for Christ" and on the front was a drawing of a cross. He was surprised at times when people began to throw things at him, but on the other hand, he met a lot of lovely people on the way and pastors would invite him to their church and show their hospitality.

Dr. Gober graduated from Georgia Tech with a degree in Systems Engineering and then set up computer systems for HCA. He then became interested in the human computer, our body, and decided to further his education. He took courses at UGA in English, Biology and Chemistry. He also attended Pharmacy school as a prelude to Medical School in 1980 at the Medical College of Georgia in Augusta. He was with Kaiser Permanente in San Francisco where he completed his first year of surgery and then went to Cooperstown, New York, to complete his second year of Surgery, moving on to Boston, Massachussetts, for four years of Urology at Tufts Medical School.

Dr. Gober is in the Georgia Army National Guard and saw active duty in Germany for 1 1/2 years, the Persian Gulf, Texas, and was deployed to Iraq.

Susan was born in Jacksonville, Florida and graduated with a B.S. in Biology and a B.A. in Psychology. In 1976 she sang with the International Choral Festival and the group took the bronze medal. They had the pleasure of singing at the Sistene Chapel, the Catacombs and on Easter Sunday, sang before the Pope who gave them his blessing. Susan joined the Peace Corp, taught school for a year in upstate New York and for three years in a Boston Inter-magnet school.

Susan and Dr. Gober met in a Doc in a Box. How many of you remember these small offices where walk-ins and emergencies were seen and then referred to a hospital if need be? They were married in October of 1986. They have lived in many places and when they received a letter from Dr. Richard J. Turner asking them if they would like to practice urology in Rabun County, they were ready to do this. Oddly enough, I typed the letter dictated by Dr. Turner asking them to come here. They bought a pickup truck, packed all their belongings in it and moved here in 1990. Even stranger, I am now helping Dr. Gober in his office on Monday afternoons, so our friendship continues. Dr. Gober and Dr. Ezzard practice Urology in the Tiger Clinic and also see patients in Toccoa.

Susan and her children are very interested in creative cooking and she shares some of her recipes with us now. This is a most interesting family and I am glad our association continues.

Forgotten Cookies

3/4 teaspoon sugar
1/2 teaspoon vanilla extract
3/4 cup chocolate morsels
2 egg whites
pinch of salt
1/2 cup nuts (optional)

Preheat oven to 350 degrees. Beat egg whites until stiffened. They must be foamy white and hard. Mix sugar and vanilla into egg whites slowly while beating them. Turn beater off, and add chocolate chips and nuts if desired. Drop small spoonfuls onto a cookie sheet covered in foil. Place cookie sheet in oven and TURN OVEN OFF. Leave overnight or 6-8 hours without opening oven door. Makes about two dozen cookies. Remember to make spoon drops small. You can double the recipe, but make sure you can fit them all in your oven.

Banana / Pear Bread

1 1/2 cups sugar
1/2 cup margarine softened
2 eggs
3 to 4 medium ripe bananas - mashed
1 Asian pear finely chopped
1/2 cup milk
1 tsp. vanilla
2 1/2 cups self-rising flour

Preheat oven to 350 degrees. Grease bottom and sides of 2 8-inch loaf pans. Mix sugar, margarine, eggs, vanilla, bananas and milk until blended thoroughly. Add flour and pear. Pour into loaf pans. Bake for one hour or until brown. Place tin foil on top for the last 10 minutes to avoid over-browning tops. This is an awesome breakfast or something great to take to a friend as a treat.

Veggie Quiche

2 pet Ritz Deep-Dish pie shells
12-14 eggs
1 oz cheddar cheese
veggies (red, yellow & green bell peppers)
ham, onions (optional)

Heat oven to 350 degrees. Thaw pie shells. Scramble eggs. Grate cheese. Gradually pour egg mixture into pie crusts adding veggies and cheese at the same time. You can put anything into a quiche depending on what your family desires. Using different colors makes the meal more appealing. Bake for one hour or until done. Serve with a tossed salad and bread.

This recipe serves more than a family of eight. You can use your favorite veggies. The number of eggs is actually determined by the amount of your ingredients in the quiche. Our children tend to eat what we grow in the garden. It's a great way for kids to start enjoying vegetables.

May, 2006

Across the Table from

Joan & Bud Attonito

*H*ave you ever met someone for the first time and felt you had known them all along? That was the feeling I had when I visited with Joan and Bud Attonito. They made me feel right at home as we sat over Irish Soda Bread with our coffee and tea. This was quite appropriate as it happened to be St. Patrick's Day.

The Attonitos are from Long Island, New York, and they moved to Tiger, Georgia in 1999. Bud and Joan met while they both attended Buffalo State Teacher's College. Both are retired teachers, and Bud did some substituting when they first moved to Rabun County.

Bud and Joan have two sons. John, a jeweler, lives in Glade Park, Colorado. This suits his lifestyle as he enjoys the great outdoors. David lives in Grayson, Georgia, with his wife and five-year-old daughter, Gracie. One time while visiting with David, the Attonitos toured the surrounding countryside and decided to give up the hustle-bustle of New York and settle in the beautiful mountains. David is an artist, and I enjoyed his lovely works of art displayed throughout his parents' home. There was one painting of a blue jay perched on a water spigot catching a drop of water in his beak. I was smitten with this painting and spent some time just enjoying it and appreciating his talent.

Joan proudly showed me a lovely handmade quilt in their bedroom. She won the quilt in a raffle. It was made by one of the Attonito's very dear friends. Joan so wanted to win this quilt as it had some green in it, which would fit beautifully with the decor of their bedroom, and guess what? She won the raffle.

The couple is very active in St. Helena's Catholic Church. The church is a large part of their lives, and they enjoy both the social life with church friends and working with others on church committees and projects. One of their favorite activities is teaching an English as a Second Language class one evening a week for Mexican adults. Bud also serves as co-chairman of the Relay For Life team the church sponsors. They both will soon begin training with CASA (Court Approved Special Advocates) to meet the needs of children who have been abused in the home.

Bud loves to write and had two poems published in *Expressions from North Georgia,* a book published by the Georgia Heritage Center for the Arts. I read the poems, and artistic talent certainly runs in the family. He also writes fairy tales and short stories.

The Attonitos are also active in the community and have enjoyed making many new friends in the area. They love entertaining, as they both enjoy people and cooking. Joan especially likes to make different kinds of cookies. Bud makes a wonderful spaghetti sauce which he named for his mother. The recipe is included here, along with his Orange-Chocolate Biscotti.

Needless to say, I spent a very enjoyable afternoon with Bud and Joan and am happy I was afforded the opportunity to meet them.

I had a hard time selecting the recipes I wanted to include. They all looked so good, but here are a few for you to enjoy. Buon Appetito!

Artichoke Pie

Pastry for two crust pie
2 pkgs. frozen artichoke hearts
3/4 lb. shredded mozzarella
8 large eggs
3 tbs. olive oil
1/2 c. grated Pecorino Romano
1 tsp. garlic powder
Salt and pepper to taste

Slice the artichoke hearts and add garlic powder, salt, and pepper. Saute in olive oil until defrosted. Do not overcook. Mix all ingredients except hearts. Mix well. Add hearts when cooled. Fill shell and cover. Bake at 350 degrees for 1 to 1 1/4 hour until golden brown.

Rafaella's Marinara Sauce

1/4 c. olive oil
1/2 medium onion, sliced thin
3 cloves minced garlic
28 oz. can diced tomatoes (packed in juice, not puree)
3 tbs. parsley
1 tbs. oregano
1/4 c. grated Romano cheese (or another hard grating cheese of your choice)
salt, pepper, to taste
crushed red pepper flakes (optional)

In a large, deep skillet, saute onions in oil until translucent. Add and saute garlic, but do not allow to brown. Add tomatoes with juice. Bring to simmer. Add all other ingredients. Simmer for 15 to 20 minutes.

Irish Soda Bread

Preheat oven to 350 degrees.
Butter two 8" cake pans.
Sift together:
4 c. flour
1 c. sugar
1 tsp. baking soda
2 tsp. baking powder
1 tsp. salt

Add and combine 1 tb. caraway seeds and 1 c. golden raisins. Break up 4 oz. softened butter. Cut into dry mixture. Mix together 2 eggs and 1 1/4 c. buttermilk. Stir in with fork. Turn dough out onto floured surface. Knead only until well-combined. (Note: Flour hands; dough is very sticky). Divide dough into two portions. Shape each portion into a round ball. Place one in each buttered pan. Bake 45 minutes, until golden brown and toothpick comes out clean.

Lemon Soup

1 c. orzo pasta
3 (14 1/2 oz.) cans fat-free chicken broth
2 egg whites
1 egg yolk
juice of one lemon

Bring broth to boil. Add orzo and cook to desired tenderness. Beat egg whites until foamy. Add egg yolk and lemon juice. Pour egg mixture into broth and orzo. Whisk to combine. (May use equivalent amount of an egg substitute product in place of egg whites and yolk)

Orange-Chocolate Biscotti

1/4 c. softened butter
1 1/4 c. sugar
1 tsp. baking powder
2/3 c. pistachio nuts
4 large eggs
2 c. flour
2/3 c. semi-sweet chocolate mini-chips
zest from 2 large oranges

Heat oven to 350 degrees. Lightly grease large cookie sheets. Beat butter, 1 c. sugar, orange zest and baking powder in mixer on high speed until well-blended. Beat in 3 eggs. On low speed, beat in flour. Stir in chips and nuts. Dough will be very sticky. Divide dough into 4 portions. Form each into a 9" log. Place logs 3" apart on cookie sheets. Brush with beaten egg and sprinkle with remaining 1/4 c. sugar. Bake 20-25 minutes until golden brown. Cool 5 minutes. Remove to cutting board. Cut into 1/2" diagonal slices. Bake 15-17 minutes until crisp. Cool. Store in airtight container at room temperature up to 3 weeks. Freeze up to 3 months.

June, 2006

Across the Table from

Nettawyl & John Davis

It was a lovely spring morning when I drove to the home of Nettawyl and John Davis, but there were storm clouds overhead. We were all praying for rain, since it was so dry. When I pulled into their driveway I admired the dogwoods and azaleas. As I opened the door I was greeted by their friendly Sheltie, Prince, who led me to the front door very gently, a good host indeed. Now, if you had a Prince living in your house he would rule the roost - as he does in this household.

Nettawyl and John are so easy to talk to and I always enjoy being with them. We all are members of the Clayton Baptist Church and sing in the Sanctuary Choir and share many interests such as golf and traveling. They play golf at the county course, Kingwood and Sky Valley and especially like traveling to North Carolina to play Pinehurst.

Nettawyl was born in Worth County, Georgia and the family moved to Albany when she was in high school. John was an Albany native and the couple met in high school there. John attended North Georgia College in Dahlonega and then entered the Air Force. Even though they dated in high school, each went a separate way and married someone else. John had three children and Nettawyl had one child by the time they reunited 10 years later and married. They have one child together and family scattered around the country. Naturally, they are proud of their four grandchildren and two great grandchildren.

Before moving to Clayton, the Davises vacationed at Kingwood to play golf. There, they fell in love with the area, as does everyone who has the opportunity to visit our beautiful mountains. They also stayed at the Old Clayton Inn and were given the bridal suite for being the youngest couple there. Visiting with friends in Highlands periodically and becoming familiar with the area, they decided on Rabun County as the place they wanted to live. They have had a home here now for 10 years.

Both have a very active church life. John is on the board of deacons and Nettawyl is director of Women On Missions. They enjoy volunteering at the desk at the Ministry Activities Center of the church and she also volunteers with the hospital auxiliary. The couple enjoys being together in the Victory Sunday School Class, are avid golfers and love to travel. Nettawyl especially loves watching Braves baseball.

John retired from the Civil Service and was with the Marine Logistics Corp in Albany. Nettawyl retired as Vice President of First Union Bank, formerly Georgia Federal Bank, after over 30 years of service.

As we sat chatting in their lovely family room, Nettawyl, who loves to cook, served apple pie, warm from the oven. I asked for a small piece and instantly regretted it after one bite: it was so good. It is such a simple recipe to be that good. The recipe is included in those she shares with us. Imagine this with some of John's special ice cream, which is also included.

Well, the rain we had prayed for finally broke in the way of a thunderstorm. Prince came inside and enjoyed being with all of us as we chatted. What a lovely way to spend a morning - listening to the much-needed rain outside and feeling cozy and welcome with friends and Prince. Thank you both for an enjoyable morning. Now to the recipes.

Sweet Potato Souffle

Begin with 3 cups of sweet potatoes that have been peeled, sliced, boiled, drained and mashed. Mix with 3/4 - 1 c. sugar (not a full cup), 1/2 tsp. salt, 2 beaten eggs, 1/2 stick margarine, 1/2 c. milk, 1 tsp. vanilla. After mixing, pour into buttered casserole dish. Top with: 1 c. light brown sugar, 1/3 c. flour, 1 c. chopped nuts, 1/2 stick melted margarine. Bake 35 minutes at 350 degrees.

Quick Hot Apple Pie

Peel 2 apples, cut in strips and layer in bottom of pie pan. Sprinkle cinnamon over apples as desired. Cut sides off 4 slices of white bread. Cut each slice into 4 rectangles. Place these over apples. Mix 1 stick real butter (melted), 1 c. sugar and 1 egg. Pour over pie. Cook 25-30 minutes at 350 degrees.

Mrs. Hardenburgh's $1,000 Prize Recipe for Chicken

6 chicken breasts or strips
1 stick butter or oleo
1/4 tsp. rosemary
1 small can mushrooms
juice of 1/2 lemon
salt, black pepper, paprika
1/4 tsp. basil
1/2 c. chopped onions
1/2 c. slivered almonds
1 can cream of mushroom soup
1 c. rice, cooked separately

Place chicken in baking dish. Sprinkle with salt, pepper and paprika. In another skillet, melt butter or oleo. Add all other ingredients except rice and pour over chicken. Cook 1 hour and 15 minutes in 350 degree oven. Cook rice separately. When ready to serve, lift chicken out, pour gravy over rice. Serve breast of chicken on mound of rice.

John's Ice Cream

4 eggs
1 c. condensed milk
1/2 gal. milk

Mix all ingredients in large boiler. Bring to a boil, remove from stove, cool, and put into refrigerator until cold. Mix fruit of your choice and freeze.

As with any ice cream the toppings are endless. Such a nice treat on a warm summer day.

July, 2006

Across the Table

Richard Welch

One of the things I enjoy about being associated with the Laurel is the opportunity to meet new friends. Such is the case this morning as I drive up the mountain to meet with Richard and Jill Welch. As I reach their house, named Serenity, the views are outstanding. I was greeted by the Welches, along with their registered Border Collie named Emme-Bam. She is very friendly and responds to sign language as well as the spoken word. This was remarkable as I watched her obey one hand signal after another from Jill. Now, let's not leave out their other doggie named Sassy, even though she spends most of her waking hours on "her" sofa in the living room.

Richard hails from Kalamazoo, Michigan. Jill's family moved around so much due to her father's job that it was difficult to name a particular place where she grew up. Richard and Jill were married eight years ago in Atlanta and wanted to honeymoon somewhere within driving distance. They ended up in a chalet in Sky Valley. They both have children, grandchildren, and one great grandchild, who live quite a distance from them.

A few years later they were taking a drive with no particular destination in mind. Right then and there they decided to spend their retirement years in these mountains. They saw a house, signed papers at 9:00 a.m. one day, then went home to Clearwater, Florida, and put their condo up for sale immediately. The house they chose here is in the Bell Colony of Dillard. They have enjoyed it for six years now.

You have already met Jill; she was featured in the April issue of Rabun's Laurel in a story about the Clayton Music, Literary and Visual Arts Club. She is president of the club and an accomplished violinist. But today I am interviewing Richard.

Richard was in the Army and served in Korea. He attended pharmacy school and then decided it was not what he wanted to do. He explored sales as a manager of J.C. Penney, worked for Montgomery Ward, sold wines along the way and became very knowledgeable about them. Richard just loved selling and relates to people very well. I have a feeling he could sell anything to anyone.

Richard's hobby is woodworking and he has his shop in an oversized garage he added to the house. In the kitchen of the home stands a butcher-block table he built which houses all of his knives, keeping them ready for food preparation.

Richard learned to cook out of neccessity, as his mother was not a very good cook. Through his experience selling wines he became more and more acquainted with them and their use, as they flavor food beautifully. He uses wine rather than a lot of different seasonings in his preparations. Richard also does not believe in recipes or exact measurements. We have all met someone along the way who tells us to use a pinch of this and a tad of that.

Richard loves preparing food on the grill and feels presentation is very important. He enjoys preparing dishes from pictures, not recipes. In the freezer he keeps beef, pork, chicken and fish. They are ready whenever he decides something in a magazine looks interesting.

I asked if he had any flops along the way. "Oh, yes," he said, and admitted that he is his biggest critic. He enjoys keeping dishes simple enough to prevent running to the store for a lot of ingredients and prefers fresh products.

I so enjoyed chatting over our lunch of Richard's pea soup and marinated shrimp he prepared on the grill, served over rice. Dessert was a strawberry pie made by Jill, the baker in the family. Yes, Richard, the presentation was wonderful, as was your meal. It looked like something out of a magazine. I even took some home to enjoy later, along with the lovely red rose that adorned our luncheon table.

Thank you Richard and Jill for a delightful time and affording me the opportunity of making new friends.

*Richard Welch was so pleased to be in the **Laurel** and couldn't wait to see his article but he passed away to a better place before this could be accomplished. Jill's violin helps her carry on.*

Richard's Recipes

Beer Can Chicken

1 whole chicken
1 can beer (or ginger ale, etc.)
1/4 cup olive oil

Wash chicken and pat dry. Coat with olive oil. Open beer and place on grill. Place chicken over can (in cavity). Close cover. Grill at medium heat for 2 hours. No basting or turning. Remove and eat. (no work, easy)

Pea Soup

1 ham bone with meat
1 bag dried peas, washed
1 medium potato, cubed
2 carrots, chopped
1/2 sweet onion, chopped
2 stalks celery, chopped
1 tsp. cumin
salt and pepper
water

Cover ham bone with water and bring to a boil. When it falls apart, remove and cool. Cut the meat off the bone and cube. Put ham water in refrigerator to cool 15 minutes. Add 3 glasses of ice cubes, cool another 15 minutes. Remove ice cubes and fat. Put ham water back in pan. Add cut ham, peas, vegetables and all seasonings. Cover and simmer 1 1/2 hours. Serve rustic or let cool and puree.

Chicken and Dumplings

1 chicken
1/2 cup celery
1/2 cup carrots
1 bay leaf
1/2 sweet onion
water to cover chicken
1 cup self-rising flour

Put chicken and all vegetables in a large pot. Cover with water and boil until chicken is done. Remove chicken and cut up. Put chicken back in pot. Mix flour and water (can use buttermilk) to wet dough. Using 2 spoons, spoon dough into pot. Cover and cook about 10-15 minutes. Serve. (easy)

Leg of Lamb

1 leg of lamb, deboned by butcher
garlic
1 bottle red wine
2 tsp. rosemary

With paring knife, poke about 12 slits in both sides of lamb. Sliver garlic and push into slits. Put lamb in pan, add red wine to cover, add rosemary and refrigerate 24 hours, turning 3-4 times. Drain juice and remove rosemary. Place on medium to high heat on grill and cook to desired doneness. Do not overcook. (wonderful and easy)

Grilled Shrimp on Skewers

6-8 raw shrimp per person
1 cup marinade essence
1/2 cup cider vinegar
1/2 cup olive oil

Whisk together essence, cider vinegar and olive oil. Peel and clean shrimp. Place in zip-lock bag. Add marinade, refrigerate 1-4 hours. Put shrimp on skewers. Put on grill, medium heat, 3-5 minutes, turning (do not overcook - just until pink). Serve over rice, noodles, pasta, salad. (easy)

August, 2006

Across the Table from

Ruth Barnes

Today I am visiting with Ruth Barnes. As Ruth and I sat in her bright, sunny kitchen, we enjoyed a typical summer lunch of potato salad, chicken salad, crackers, iced tea and sweet, juicy watermelon. It reminded me of the potluck luncheons we used to have in the office, when Ruth brought her vegetable soup or potato salad. Here I was enjoying that delicious potato salad and didn't have to share it with the office staff. How good can it get? Ruth tells me she is a "from scratch" country cook. She was raised during the Depression, when folks raised a lot of their food and nothing was wasted. Everything was fresh back then and she continues to use fresh ingredients in her cooking.

Ruth was born and raised in the Dillard area of Rabun County. Her maiden name was Williams and she had three sisters and one brother, who all chose to stay in Rabun County. Ruth is the only remaining member of her immediate family.

Ruth met Roy Barnes, of Royston, when her father was supervisor of the camp Roy worked in one summer. Her father introduced the two. They started dating and married when Ruth was 16-years-old. Roy went on to work for the Gulf Oil Company for 27 years. The extended family includes three grandchildren and two great-grandchildren. Ruth has a son, Bobby, who lives in the Franklin area with his family. The Barnes are a very close-knit family, getting together for picnics, Sunday dinners and vacations. Ruth proudly showed me family pictures she keeps in her living room.

Ruth became interested in nursing when Dr. Dover came to the Health Department on Old 441 and asked some of the girls to help him by getting the shots ready. She was about 14-years-old then and stepped right up and enjoyed helping the doctor. This led to her working for several doctors in the area. One day, when she brought her mother to the emergency room, she met Dr. Richard Turner. Her mother encouraged the doctor to remain here, as there was a shortage of doctors in rural areas. Dr. Turner mentioned he could use another nurse and once again Ruth stepped up.

Ruth and I worked together in this setting for 23 years. She gave me permission to mention she is now 85 years of age and still going strong. She does all of her own housework. She especially enjoys helping the elderly patients and visiting homebound members of her church, Clayton Baptist. She is an active member of the Joy Sunday School class and a member of the Carter Miller Circle. Along with all of this, she enjoyed helping her daughter-in-law Margie at the Blue Willow Tea Room when it was on Savannah Street, and continues to help Margie and Margie's daughter Kelly at The Tree House on Main Street. Ruth presented me with a lovely teapot from The Tree House, as she knows I am a tea lover.

Prior to working with doctors, Ruth managed the theatre on Main Street, in the block where Reeves Hardware is located. During the making of "The Great Locomotive Chase," Walt Disney came to the theatre at night to review the filming done that day, affording Ruth the opportunity to chat with him. He told her of his dream to build a place where families could go and have fun together. He loved children and wanted to provide something special for them. Rising from this dream came Disneyland in

California. Mr. Disney invited Ruth and her family to visit, but he died before it happened. Ruth was an extra in the movie and met Fess Parker. Again, how good can it get?

I think it is interesting that it was Ruth's son, Bobby, who suggested the site for Dr. Turner to build his office, with other buildings to follow. Bobby played there as a child and thought the place on the hill would be just right. The Barneses showed Dr. Turner around, and he was able to purchase the land. It is the current site of Mountain Lakes Medical Center.

Ruth has given us some wonderful recipes to enjoy. We had such a good time reminiscing and speaking of the changes in the area. Thank you, Ruth, for a most pleasant afternoon.

Cumin-crusted Pork Tenderloin with bean and corn salad

1/2 cup chopped red onion
1 teaspoon grated lime zest
1/3 cup lime juice
Pork
2 tablespoons cumin seeds
3/4 teaspoons paprika
3/4 teaspoons salt
1 pork tenderloin, about 1 pound
non-stick spray
1 can (15.5 oz.) butter beans, rinsed
1 can (11 oz.) extra-sweet corn, drained
1/2 cup cilantro leaves, chopped
1/4 teaspoon ground chipotle pepper, or to taste (optional)

Marinate onion in lime zest and juice for 30 minutes in a medium bowl, to soften. Meanwhile, heat oven to 450 degrees. Wrap handle (if not heat-proof) of a large nonstick skillet with 2 layers of foil. Pork: mix cumin seeds, paprika and salt in a cup. Rub over tenderloin. Coat pork and skillet with non-stick spray. Heat skillet over medium heat. Add pork and cook, turning until nicely browned on all sides. Place in oven and roast 12 minutes, or until a meat thermometer inserted in center registers 155 degrees. Remove from oven and let stand 5 minutes before slicing. Add remaining ingredients to onions. Serve with the pork.

Poke Sallet

Gather all the sallet you can find (it cooks down). Pick 6 to 7-inch shoots. Wash and clean; swim the shoots in plenty of water in a large pot and boil until tender. Meanwhile, slice a pan of country bacon and fry out the grease. When the poke is tender, drain off the water it was cooked in, and cover it with cold water. Squeeze it out of the cold water into hot bacon grease. Salt to taste, and cook slowly until hot throughout. Serve with hot bacon and cornbread.

Fried Salt Pork

"Fat Back," "Poor Man's Chicken," or whatever. Select with care. A streak-of-lean is preferred, although many discriminating cooks use pure fat. Use thick slices, about 4 per serving. Cover with boiling water, bring to a boil, discard the salt water. Drain. Dip slices in cornmeal. Fry in hot shortening until slices are golden brown. Drain on paper towels. Serve with biscuits, gravy and sliced tomatoes.

Wilted Lettuce

Select fresh spring lettuce before it heads. Chop lettuce to fill bowl, add 3 or 4 young green onions, heads and tops, chopped fine. Cook about 6 slices of country-cured bacon until crisp. Crumble and sprinkle over lettuce. Pour hot bacon drippings over all. Serve immediately. Good with cornbread and fried potatoes.

Old Fashioned Egg Custard

3 eggs
1 cup sugar
1 cup milk
1 tablespoon vanilla
1 tablespoon flour
3 tablespoons butter or margarine
1 unbaked pie shell

Mix sugar and flour well. Add well-beaten eggs, milk, vanilla, and melted butter. Pour into unbaked pie shell and bake at 350 degrees for about 45 minutes or until center is firm. Nutmeg may be sprinkled on top.

September, 2006

Across the Table from

The Sayettas

" *I* wish they could all be California girls." This song from the Beach Boys kept going through my mind, as I was about to interview Mary Sayetta, who is indeed a California girl who is now our Georgia peach.

Mary lived in Santa Maria and was a graphic designer at Saddleback Church in Lake Forest. She worked with Rick Warren for five years. Many of you will recognize his name as the author of *The Purpose-Driven Life*. Mary helped with the artwork in his book and also freelanced for outside ministries.

Eddie Sayetta is the Associate Pastor of Worship and Music at Clayton Baptist Church. Eddie attended conferences in California, where he met Mary. At times she would attend some here on the East coast. Their friendship grew over the years until they realized they wanted to spend the rest of their lives together. It is Mary's marriage to Eddie that brought her here to Rabun County. The ceremony was held at the Clayton Baptist Church in April of 2005. The new bride was kept busy giving Eddie's house in Dillard the feminine touch.

Eddie grew up in Columbia, South Carolina, so he was already a Southern boy. He moved about as he graduated from Furman University and went on to Seminary at Southwestern in Texas. Mary continues to work in the area of graphic design, having her own business, In Faith Graphic Design. She enjoys the convenience of working out of their home.

Mary is active in volunteer work at the MAC of the church, and is a member of the Sanctuary Choir led by Eddie. She especially enjoys making visits along with Eddie and works with Habitat for Humanity. She dabbles in photography and they both love to travel, especially to see her new nephew in California. Their dream trip is to take a Carribean cruise, so she still likes to feel the sand between her toes as she walks on the beach. Mary especially enjoys the change of seasons afforded us here in the mountains and has found the people to be most friendly. Mary and Eddie both enjoy cooking and Eddie likes to bake. He loves all those neat appliances that whirl and twist around, making it fun. They entertain a lot and are wonderful hosts. Eddie uses his love of entertaining to get to know people on a more intimate basis.

One of Mary's favorite things to do is collect recipes from her favorite restaurants. She also is well-versed in the art of barbecue, as this was her dad's specialty. He was on the Elk's Barbecue team for fundraisers. Of course, Santa Maria Valley is known as the barbecue capital of the world.

I so much enjoyed my time with you, Mary and Eddie. Thanks for giving us your favorite recipes to try. We are so glad this California girl and Southern boy live here with us in Rabun County, and we wish you much happiness in the years to come.

Chipotle's Basmati Rice

It is hard to beat this rice dish, attributed to Chipotle's Executive Chef and CEO, Steve Ellis.

1 tsp. vegetable oil or butter
2 tsp. fresh cilantro
2/3 c. white basmati rice
1 c. water
1/2 tsp. salt
1 lime

In a 2 qt. heavy saucepan, heat oil or butter over low heat, stirring occasionally until melted. Add rice and lime juice, stir for 1 minute. Add water and salt, bring to a full rolling boil. At boiling, cover, turn down to simmer over low heat until rice is tender and the water is absorbed, about 25 minutes. Fluff rice with fork.

Basmati (bahs-MAH-tee) is a long-grained rice, with a fine texture. It can be found in Middle Eastern and Indian markets, as well as some supermarkets.   (serves 4)

Macaroni Grill's Gemberetti Noci E De Pino

24 jumbo shrimp, peeled and deveined,
  or substitute with chicken tenders
3 c. sliced mushrooms, 1/4 inch thick,
  washed and sliced
1 1/2 tbsp. roasted pine nuts
6 handfuls fresh spinach leaves
6 c. cooked vermicelli pasta
4 tbsp. butter
2 tbsp. fresh garlic, minced
lemon butter sauce
1 tbsp. shallots, minced
1 tbsp. fresh garlic, minced
1/2 c. dry white wine
1 c. heavy cream
1/2 c. lemon juice, freshly squeezed
1/8 tsp. white pepper
1 lb. lightly salted butter, cut into tablespoons

Preheat oven to 350ª. Wash spinach and remove stems before drying leaves between paper towels. Set aside. Spread pine nuts over bottom of sheet pan and place pan in oven on top rack. Roast until golden brown, approximately 2 to 4 minutes. Remove from oven and set aside.

Peel and devein shrimp (or wash chicken tenders). Set aside. Wash and slice fresh mushrooms. Set aside. Boil pasta in large pot of water to al dente stage according to directions on package. Set aside.

Prepare lemon butter sauce: melt 1 tablespoon butter in large skillet over medium-high heat. Saute shallots and garlic until translucent. Add white wine and reduce slightly more than 1/2, whisking occasionally. Add cream and reduce by 1/2. Add lemon juice and reduce by 1/2. Add white pepper. Reduce heat to low. Add remaining butter 2 tablespoons at a time, whisking continuously after each addition to completely incorporate butter. Continue to simmer, whisking until sauce just coats spoon.

In large skillet over medium-high heat melt the 4 tablespoons of butter. Add garlic and saute until garlic is translucent. Stir in mushrooms, shrimp, and pine nuts. Saute several minutes or until shrimp are done and show color. Remove skillet from heat and gently stir in spinach. Place warm pasta on plate with shrimp mixture to the side. Pour lemon sauce over pasta, permitting a bit of sauce onto shrimp. (Makes 6)

Vegetable Fajitas

8 oz. chopped cilantro, for pesto
3 cloves garlic, for pesto
1/2 c. olive oil, for pesto
1/8 tsp. salt, or to taste, for pesto
1/8 tsp. pepper, or to taste, for pesto
2 oz. freshly-grated Parmesan cheese, for pesto
1 medium onion, sliced
1/2 tbsp. margarine
carrots, zucchini and yellow summer squash,
  cut julienne-style
broccoli and cauliflower, cut into small florets
green pepper and mushrooms, thinly sliced
snow peas, whole
juice of half a lemon
3 flour tortillas, warmed, or cooked rice
lime wedge, for garnish
pico de gallo, for condiment
guacamole, for condiment
sour cream, for condiment
shredded Cheddar cheese, for condiment
salsa, for condiment

To make pesto, put cilantro and garlic in a food processor and process until finely chopped. With machine on, gradually add olive oil. Season and blend in cheese.

Slice enough onion to equal about 1/2 cup. Saute with margarine in a small cast-iron skillet over medium-high heat. Cook past translucent stage until browned, about six to eight minutes.

Prepare about 2 cups of vegetables--the combination depends on personal taste. Cook all vegetables except mushrooms in lemon juice and 2 tablespoons of pesto over medium to medium-high heat. When almost at al dente stage, add sliced mushrooms. Continue cooking for about one minute. (The remaining pesto can be refrigerated for future use.)

Place vegetable mixture over sizzling onions, then spoon vegetable-onion mixture into center of warmed tortillas or rice. Top with condiments, to taste. (makes 8)

October, 2006

Across the Table from

Diane & Bill Bond

*S*tranger than fiction. Today I am interviewing Diane and Bill Bond. Most of you will know the lady in the story but you may not be familiar with the gentleman.

I have known Diane for many years as a friend and beautician. I introduced myself to Bill and he in turn introduced himself as Bond, Bill Bond, double-o three-and-a-half. I knew immediately that this was going to be a fun interview. We sat on their lovely front porch while drinking our coffee as we talked.

Diane was raised in Scaly, North Carolina, and lived there until she was thirteen, when the family moved to Rabun Gap. Her parents were Otis and Hattie Lee Burnette. She has two brothers, Vernon and Lamar, and three sisters, Donna, Brenda and Sandra. Diane married, moved to Tiger, and had three sons, Mike, Jamie and Woody Blalock. She now has six grandchildren.

Diane graduated from North Georgia Tech as a beautician and has been in the business for thirty-three years. A shop was built into the house and she remained there for twenty-seven years. As time went by and the children married and moved into places of their own, Diane felt the house was just too big for her and put it up for sale. In the meantime, she built a smaller house on Rogers Street in Clayton and took up her business there.

Bill was born in Milford, Massachusetts in 1936. He served in the Army for thirteen years. When Bill married,

he moved to Pembroke Pines, Florida, near Hollywood. His wife died at age forty-nine, despite the fact that Bill donated one of his kidneys to her. Being left alone with four boys to raise, he sold his pet supply business and stayed home with the boys. Two grandchildren have now been added to his family. He had visited friends in the Warwoman community and decided it was time to move to the mountains. He wanted a house in the mountains, but not on top of a mountain. When he saw Diane's house in Tiger with its large yard, he knew it was the house for him. He bought the house in 2005. Diane continued business in Tiger, renting her shop until she was able to move into her new surroundings.

But let's go back a bit before we learn the "rest of the story." In October 2003 Diane was putting the magazines in her shop in order and she noticed each one mentioned breast cancer month. They stressed the importance of everyone performing self-examinations each month. Since Diane had not practiced this, she decided to follow through in the shower that night and discovered a lump in her breast. She made an appointment with the doctor for the next week. In November of 2003 she was diagnosed with breast cancer and underwent surgery, along with eight chemo treatments and thirty-three radiation treatments. During this, Diane allowed herself to close her shop the week she was going through treatment but worked the rest of the time. Although uncomfortable at times, she was so dedicated to her customers that she kept going. I remember all the cute hats she wore when she lost her hair, but she never lost her spirit. Her attitude was wonderful, never complaining and she gives credit to the many prayers and to the support of her many caring friends. The treatments continued for one year. Now the good news--three years later she has been pronounced cancer-free.

Now back to the "rest of the story." Diane moved into her new house in 2006, but was not happy in her surroundings. She missed her shop in Tiger and her many friends. She decided she wanted to move back to her shop in her old house. In the meantime, Bill missed hearing this lady talk and laugh with her customers. He also missed visiting with Diane while she enjoyed her lunch in the gazebo he built.

When Diane moved into her new house, he invited her over to a dinner, their first date. He invited her back to dinner the next week- and asked her to marry him. By this time Diane also realized just how much fun they had together and knew she wanted to spend the rest of her life with this gentleman who bought her house. Bill moved her shop back to Tiger and renovated it. He loved working on it and it is lovely. Now you tell me--is this not "stranger than fiction?" They married on May 27th in the Tiger house with family and grandchildren attending.

Now to the recipes: Bill cooks on the days Diane works and she cooks for him when she is off. Isn't that a great arrangement? Bill especially likes to cook on the gas grille and he is interested in Diane's Southern cooking.

Thank you Dianne and Bill for such a nice interview.

Diane's Hush Puppies

3 cups self-rising corn meal
2 cups plain flour
3 eggs
grated onion

Add sweet milk to mixing consistency. Mix well and drop from teaspoon into hot oil. Enjoy.

Diane's Devils Food Cream Cheese Delight

1 box Duncan-Hines German chocolate cake mix
1 cup chopped nuts-pecans or nuts of your choice
1 cup coconut
1 box powdered sugar
1 8-ounce cream cheese
1 stick melted margarine

Sprinkle bottom of greased 9x12" pan with coconut and nuts. Mix cake mix per directions and pour on top of nuts and coconut. Mix cream cheese, sugar and melted margarine. Pour on top of cake mixture. Do not stir. Bake at 350 degrees for about 50-55 minutes.

Chinese-style Sweet and Sour Pork Chops

For marinade
1/2 cup soy sauce
1/4 cup hoisin sauce
1/4 cup white vinegar
1/4 cup honey
1/4 cup pineapple juice
2 garlic cloves, pressed
3 tablespoons peanut or vegetable oil
6 pork loin or rib chops, each 3/4 to 1 inch thick

Combine the marinade ingredients in a non-reactive container and mix well. Add the pork chops, cover the container and refrigerate for 1 to 2 hours.

Preheat the grill for ten to fifteen minutes, with all the burners on high. Once the grill is hot, turn one burner off and turn the others to medium. Drain the marinade from the container and discard it. Place the pork chops over the burner that is turned off. Close the grill's lid and cook the chops for twenty-five or thirty minutes, turning them once.

Serve the pork chops hot off the grill. Serves six.

November, 2006

Across the Table from

Cat Wheeler

*R*eaders of Rabun's Laurel will recognize the name of Tony Wheeler, the editor of the magazine. You enjoy reading his columns as I do, but today I am interviewing his wife, Catherine, who prefers to be called Cat. Cat was born in Chelsea, Massachusetts, and lived in New Hampshire for awhile, and then she decided to move to Atlanta in 1975. She met Tony in their place of employment, the Bosch Corporation, and married him a year later.

Cat has a son, Robert, who resides in Hartford, Connecticut, and a daughter, Chris, who lives here in Rabun County. She has six grandchildren. Cat and Tony visited friends here in Rabun County and enjoyed camping in the Warwoman area. Once you have visited this area, who can resist wanting to live here? So they loaded up a friend's pickup truck and made the move to Rabun County and have been here now for about twenty years. They have never regretted it for one minute.

Tony enjoys golf and Cat enjoys fishing, crocheting, and is an animal lover. Their household consists of two cats, a fifteen-pound black cat named Spanky and a Calico named Buttercup. Since they are indoor cats, when Cat brings groceries into the house, Spanky picks Buttercup up by the scruff of the neck to keep her from running outside.

I first met Cat at Woodridge Hospital, where she was employed in the Dietary Department. When the hospitals merged, she went up to Ridgecrest Hospital in the same department. She later began her own cleaning service, but when arthritis set in, realized she would have to give it up and is now a homemaker.

I knew Cat was well-versed in the art of cooking and asked if she would share some of her recipes with us. This being the month of Thanksgiving, I asked if she followed any traditions handed down by her family. She remembers the whole family going to her mother's house to join with aunts, uncles and cousins, and that they always had such a good time. Now folks live so far apart, we do not carry on these traditions as much as we did in the past. It used to be "over the river and through the woods to Grandmother's house we go," but now it is hop in the car, drive to the airport, check your luggage (which is getting more and more difficult), and travel during the airport's most-traveled time of the year.

I remember when my mother and father would take me to Gimbel's Thanksgiving Day parade, when we welcomed Santa Claus to the city of Philadelphia. "Billy Penn" stood in the background and we stamped our feet and clapped our hands to keep warm, but it was a wondrous sight. Then we would go to my Aunt Jennie's house to partake of her wonderful dinner. She always prepared two turkeys, as we all stayed for cold turkey sandwiches in the evening. I enjoyed this more than the cooked dinner. You take two slices of white bread, fill one with turkey and spread jellied cranberry sauce on top, or coleslaw, covered by the other piece of bread. Oh my, was it good. Many of us are by ourselves now as the holidays approach, with family living far away. Some of our friends and loved ones are now living in a better place, but you don't have to be alone. Start your own tradition. Invite others who are in the same boat as you to your house. They may bring a side dish if they choose and this act of kindness will grow with others joining in the next year, taking turns at each house.

Now to Cat's recipes: she likes to use fresh vegetables when available and always tries to plan well-balanced dinners. Tony's specialty is chili, but not for Thanksgiving.

They also enjoy cooking on the grill year-round. Cat's mother always made bread stuffing with poultry seasoning and giblet gravy, as my mother did. It wasn't until we both moved south that we ever had cornbread stuffing outside the turkey. Our bread stuffing was always packed inside the bird. At Christmas, Cat remembers stringing cranberries and popcorn for the tree. There are many happy memories of holidays past, but now we can make our own memories. I so enjoyed visiting with you Cat, and learning more about you. It is always fun.

Turkey Stuffing Mix

2-3 loaves day-old bread
2 tbsp. bacon grease
small onion, finely chopped
small bell pepper, finely chopped
2 cloves garlic, finely chopped
1 tbsp. parsley
1 tbsp. paprika
4 tbsp. poultry seasoning
3 16 oz. cans chicken stock

In skillet, fry onion, bell pepper and garlic in bacon grease. Meanwhile, break bread into bite-sized pieces and place in mixing bowl. Mix skillet preparation and all other ingredients with bread, adding chicken stock last. (2 cans for stuffing, 1 can reserved for cooking turkey.) Add chicken stock slowly; bread needs to be moist but not soupy. (You may have leftover stock.) -See next recipe...

Thanksgiving Turkey

10-12 lb. Butterball turkey
First, check bird's cavities for packaged giblets, etc. - you don't want any surprises later. Wash and clean turkey thoroughly using warm water. I like to scrub the bird using table salt as an abrasive. Place stuffing mix in turkey. Tuck tail of turkey into stuffed cavity. Cross turkey legs and tie with string to keep stuffing mix in place. Place turkey in roasting pan and add one can of chicken stock. Cover pan with lid and bake at 375-400 degrees for one hour. Lower heat to 350 degrees and cook until golden brown (2-4 hours).

Yankee Apple Pie

2 9-inch pie crusts
6 Roman Beauty apples, peeled,
    cored and sliced into wedges
1/2 c. brown sugar (light or dark)
1/2 c. granulated sugar
1/2 tbsp. butter
1/2 tsp. cinnamon
2 tsp. milk
2 or 3 slices of your favorite cheese

Mix apple wedges, sugars, butter and cinnamon in a bowl. Pour into one 9-inch crust. Cover with second crust and crimp edges of the crusts together. Using a fork or knife, puncture top crust 4-6 times. Place pie in 350-degree oven and bake 45 minutes or until golden brown. Halfway through baking, sprinkle milk on top of pie. When pie is done, remove from oven and add slices of cheese to top; I prefer cheddar. Serve hot.

December, 2006

Across the Table from

The Barn Inn
Jan & Nancy

What a lovely, peaceful setting for a stay at a bed and breakfast. I am speaking of The Barn Inn at Lake Rabun. It sits atop a point of land directly across from the lake. But let me start at the beginning. The building was built as a horse barn in 1920 by Samuel Candler Dobbs.

Built of rock and timber, it has a concrete floor, which is most unusual. It served as a lodging of different sorts, and went through a succession of owners. Folk named Evans did a good part of the remodeling, after which it was then purchased by Randy Corbin and Charles Bryson in the late 1990s. Major renovations then took place on the floors and beams, along with the windows and barn doors. It even served as a private residence for a time.

Jan Timms and Nancy Gribble purchased the building in December of 2005 and opened their bed and breakfast this past April. They had traveled the East coast, stopping at B and B's along the way, and this furthered their desire to have one of their own.

As you step into the foyer, it leads up a few steps into the dining room. This is fully furnished with two dining room tables, dishes, silver, crystal and linens. Almost all of the furniture in the inn came from Jan and Nancy's household, along with antiques from family members. The only things they had to purchase were pictures and lamps. From the steps leading from the foyer, one steps into the sitting room with the large stone fireplace. It was

there we sat over our coffee, along with Apricot Nectar Cake, for which Jan gives us the recipe today. The many high windows to the front and back of the inn afford lots of light and, as the sky changes, so does the lighting in the room. To the right of the foyer is the common room. This is the only room that houses a TV and a radio, providing a peaceful atmosphere. It is here that guests can meet and chat and get to know one another better.

There are five lovely appointed bedrooms. Each has its own bath with marble vanities and is well lighted. Guests may even choose the weight of their pillows. The sheets are high count cotton and ironed if called for. Jan likes to iron--imagine that.

Both Jan and Nancy are from the corporate world and lived in Atlanta for a time. They grew tired of dealing with traffic on a daily basis and decided they wanted a more peaceful way of life. That is when they began to look at property to fulfill their dream of having their own B and B. Now let us come to the kitchen, a most important part in running this type of business. Oh my, it has the required three-bowl sink, two commercial dishwashers, a range, and a pantry. I always said when I was growing up that I would have a pantry filled with pickles and olives. They were definitely included on these shelves, along with all kinds of staples which Jan and Nancy shop for once a month.

When reservations are made, they ask guests about special dietary needs and if they are celebrating a special occasion. If so, Jan and Nancy are glad to make it special by ordering flowers and champagne to be served in the guests' room. They also provide coolers in the foyer in case couples would prefer to bring their wine. Coffee is ready at seven o'clock each morning. Guests choose the time to enjoy breakfast and they have a wide variety of food to choose from. The favorite is French toast, which is made the night before. By the time the guests leave, the hosts feel they are friends. They even make arrange-ments for them for dinner, hiking, and excursions to enjoy the different shops and sights in town. The inn is a continuing work in progress. Jan and Nancy are planting many bulbs to bloom in season around the lovely patio area and deck.

Thank you ladies for a nice visit!

Cheese and Spinach Puffs

1-10 oz. package frozen chopped spinach
1/2 cup chopped onion
2 eggs, slightly beaten
1/2 cup Parmesan cheese
1/2 cup shredded cheese
1/2 cup blue cheese salad dressing
1/2 cup melted butter
1/4 tsp. garlic powder
1 cup Bisquick

In saucepan, combine spinach and onion; cook according to spinach package directions. Drain well, pressing out all liquid. Combine eggs, cheeses, salad dressing, butter and garlic powder. Add spinach mixture and Bisquick; mix well. Cover and chill; shape dough into one-inch balls. Chill, covered, until serving time. Place chilled puffs on baking sheet and bake at 350 degrees 10 to 12 minutes. Serve warm. Makes about 60 puffs.

After shaping, balls may be frozen. Bake frozen puffs for 12 to 15 minutes.

Salmon Ball

1 large can salmon
8 oz. cream cheese
2 tbsp. freshly squeezed lemon juice
4 green onions, minced
3 tbsp. horseradish
1 tsp. Worcestershire sauce
1/2 cup chopped pecans
3 tbsp. minced fresh parsley
several dashes of cayenne pepper

Drain salmon, remove skin and bones, and flake with a fork. With mixer, chip cream cheese and blend in lemon juice, onion, horseradish, Worcestershire sauce and cayenne pepper. When well blended, stir in flaked salmon and pecans. Line a small bowl with plastic wrap and pack mixture in tightly. Cover and chill at least several hours or overnight. Unmold and roll in parsley. Serve with your choice of crackers.

Apricot Nectar Cake

For cake:
1 box yellow cake mix
3 oz. lemon jello
3/4 cup vegetable oil
4 eggs
3/4 cup apricot nectar
2 tbsp. lemon extract

Combine all ingredients and pour into well-greased and floured Bundt pan. Bake at 350 degrees for one hour.

For icing:
1 1/2 cups powdered sugar
juice of two lemons

Mix sugar and juice together. While cake is still warm, poke small holes in top of cake and pour icing over cake. (This is Jan's mother's recipe and the cake we enjoyed during our interview.)

Butterscotch Pie
From Tracy McCoy

1 1/2 cups packed brown sugar
4 tablespoons cornstarch
3 tablespoons all-purpose flour
2 cups milk
3 egg yolks
2 tablespoons butter
1 teaspoon vanilla extract
1 (9 inch) pie shell, baked

Put your pie shell in the oven and bake according to the directions on it. In a double boiler, whisk together the brown sugar, flour, and cornstarch. Add just enough milk to make a paste. Mix in beaten egg yolks, and then add the remainder of the milk. Cook slowly, stirring constantly; when thick, remove from heat. Add butter or margarine and 1 teaspoon vanilla. Pour the filling into the baked pie shell.

Hazel's Chocolate Gravy
From Tracy McCoy

1 cup of flour
1 1/2 cup of sugar
3 heaping Tbls of cocoa
Mix dry ingredients together in sauce pan
add 1 1/2 cup water and 1 cup of milk

Bring to boil over medium heat. Remove and serve over hot buttery biscuits with sausage or bacon. YUMMY!

Strawberry Pie
From Nikki McCall

1 graham cracker crust
1 (8oz). tub of Cool Whip
1 (8oz). block or tub of Strawberry cream cheese
1/3 cup of sugar

Mix ingredients together in a bowl. Spread into pie crust. You can top with strawberry pie filling or fresh strawberries if you wish.Refrigerate overnight. That's it. It's pretty simple, and very good!!

Magic Bars
From Nikki McCall

3 1/2 cups graham cracker crumbs
1 (8 oz) can sweetened condensed milk
1 bag milk chocolate morsels
1 bag sweetened coconut
1 cup chopped pecans (optional)
1 stick butter

In 9 X 13 inch baking dish pour graham cracker crumbs as bottom layer. Melt butter and drizzle over crumbs. Mash in with a fork to coat crumbs with butter. Layer chocolate chips, coconut and pecans until you have used a bag of each. Evenly pour condensed milk over the entire mixture and bake at 350 degrees until golden brown. Slice in 2 inch squares.

Sawdust Salad
From John Shivers

This recipe makes a great salad but it's also a great dessert. It's made in 3 stages, so it's necessary to start 8-10 hours before time to serve. It looks fantastic when presented in a clear glass footed trifle bowl where you can see the ingredients and the layers, but you can use an ordinary casserole dish just as easily.

STEP 1:
1 small box lemon Jello
1 small box orange Jello
2 cups hot water
1 ½ cups cold water
1 #2 can crushed pineapple, drained; save the juice
2 or 3 bananas cut into chunks
½ cup chopped pecans
Small package of miniature marshmallows

Dissolve the Jello with the hot water, then add cold water and the remainder of the ingredients. Place the thick, soupy mixture into the container you plan to serve in and place in the refrigerator to congeal until it is firm to the touch.

STEP 2:
1 cup of pineapple juice
¾ cup of sugar
2 tbs. cornstarch
2 eggs well-beaten.

Beat eggs first until light yellow and frothy, then add the pineapple juice, sugar and cornstarch. Cook in a double boiler over medium heat, stirring constantly, until the mixture has thickened to a loose custard consistency. Spread this mixture while still hot over the congealed Jello mixture and immediately return to the refrigerator.

STEP 3:
3 oz. package cream cheese, softened
Medium to large container of Cool Whip
Grated mild cheddar cheese
Whole pecans

Beat the cream cheese until soft and workable, then add Cool Whip. As the two blend, a stiff topping mixture will emerge. Spread this over the custard layer of the congealed mixture. Garnish with pecans and grated cheese. Return to the refrigerator until time to serve.

Carolina Pound Cake
From Sally Wilson

3 1/4 c flour
1/2 lb (2 sticks) butter
1/2 t baking powder
1/2 c shortening
1/2 t salt
5 eggs
2 t vanilla
3 c sugar
1 c milk

Cream, butter, sugar and shortening. Sift flour and baking powder together. Add alternately to creamed mixture with milk. Beat til incorporated and add vanilla. Pour mixture into a greased and floured tube or Bundt pan. Bake 1 hr 25 min at 355°

January, 2007

Across the Table from

Sadie Owens and the Ladies of the Ivy Hill Baptist Church

After picking up some chocolate bars that were on sale, I walked down one of the aisles in CVS. Coming up the aisle toward me was a friendly lady who smiled. I didn't know if she was smiling at me or my supply of four large Hershey bars, so I made a remark about feeling better now that I had my supply of my favorite candy once more. We started to chat and in the course of conversation she invited me to one of the fellowship meals at Ivy Hill Baptist Church, which are held on the first and third Sunday of every month. Her name was Sadie Owens and I gladly accepted the offer. One could say this was a chance meeting but I don't think so. My son calls these meetings God-incidences rather than coincidences and I agree this was the case when I met Sadie.

We chatted on the phone later to set the date for my visit. When the publisher of Rabun's Laurel, Tracy McCoy, heard of my plans she asked if she could go with me. In a later phone call I asked Sadie if we could join her in her worship service as well. Always thinking ahead for my column in the magazine

I asked if she thought some of the ladies of the church would like to share some of their recipes with me. She said she was sure they would and would have them bring them to the church when I visited.

So last Sunday found Tracy and me heading for the Ivy Hill Baptist Church. When I told everyone in my church where I was going, they all wanted to come along with me. The sanctuary is large and is beautifully decorated, as is the fellowship hall. There is a large foyer where folks may sit and chat before and after the service. There is a well-equipped kitchen with all the equipment for cooking a wonderful dinner.

Tracy and I joined the members for Sunday school and the church service which followed. We were made to feel most welcome and were graciously acknowledged from the pulpit. I already knew many of the members so I enjoyed seeing and chatting with them again. Two offerings were taken. The first was where everyone gave $3.00--one for the Father, one for the Son, and one for the Holy Spirit. This is a special offering to help those in need. I thought this was an excellent idea. Then the regular tithes and offerings were taken. Afterward I enjoyed the bountiful meal with those I knew and the new friends

I made. Many members brought their recipes and I thank the ladies of the church for doing this. Tracy took pictures and we just had a wonderful time sharing food, talking about the blessings our Lord and Savior has given us as we broke bread together. I would like to thank all the ladies, gentlemen and children for showing us such a warm welcome. Life can be so much more interesting when you open up to meeting and chatting with someone new. You never know where this will lead. Thank you Sadie--and to think this all started over a few candy bars. Who said chocolate bars are not good for you?

Mom's Baked Potato and Chili Casserole
by Lou Ann Cunningham

3 medium baking potatoes
1 (8 oz.) container sour cream
2 tbsp. freeze dried chives
2 small jars Bush's Chili with beans
1 (8 oz.) pkg. shredded cheddar cheese
Salt and pepper to taste

Preheat oven to 350 degrees. Bake potatoes ahead so they will be cool and easy to handle. They need to be cooked until fork-tender. In a large bowl mash potatoes, sour cream and chives together. In an 8" x 8" or 9" x 9" square baking dish, put in potato mixture and top with cheddar cheese. Bake this in a 350-degree oven until cheese is melted and bubbly. This recipe is a family favorite.

Baptist Pound Cake
by Hattie Fortson

3 c. sugar
2 sticks butter
5 eggs
1 c. milk
3 c. flour
1/2 tsp. baking powder

Cream butter and sugar until smooth. Add eggs one at a time, beating well after each egg. Mix baking powder with flour and sift together. Alternate with flour and milk. Pour in greased and floured pan. Bake one hour and 15 minutes until golden brown.

Old Fashioned Tea Cakes
by Willa Mae Sanford

1 stick butter
1 egg
1 3/4 c. self rising flour
1 c. sugar
2 tbsp. milk
1/2 tsp. vanilla

Cream butter, sugar, egg, milk and vanilla. Sift flour. Add to creamed mixture. Chill. Cut and bake in 375-degree oven for about eight minutes.

Baked Beans
by Mary Mance

1 lb. ground beef
1 onion, chopped fine
1 bell pepper, chopped fine
3 (15 oz.) cans pork and beans
3/4 c. firmly packed light brown sugar
2 tbsp. prepared mustard
2 tbsp. Worcestershire
2 c. ketchup

In a large skillet over medium heat, brown ground beef with onion and pepper. Drain. In a large bowl combine the pork and beans, brown sugar, mustard, Worcestershire sauce and ketchup. Mix well. Stir in the ground beef mixture. Put in crockpot and cook on low for 2 1/2 to 3 hours. Makes 12 servings. Good to take to church for dinner.

February, 2007 - *More from Jean Emhart*

A TRIBUTE TO THE LEMON

"*Lemon tree very pretty and the lemon flower is sweet - but the fruit of the lemon is impossible to eat.*" Now what other fruit can you name that has a song written about it? This particular one was written by Will Holt and made popular by Peter, Paul and Mary in 1962.

I began to think of the many ways in which the lemon is used and found so many that I thought I would pay tribute to this wonderful fruit. If I do not have flowers to enjoy, I use a bowl of lemons for decoration. They also smell so fresh and clean.

Medicinal: Did you know the lemon has many uses? How about a teaspoon of lemon and a teaspoon of honey for a cold or lemon-flavored cough drops? Years ago a doctor suggested that my mother drink the juice of a lemon in a glass of lukewarm water upon arising, to disturb the poisons in the body.

Saying: "When life hands you lemons, make lemonade."

Law: The Lemon Law protects you when you purchase a car and it does not perform in the manner expected.

Laundry: Add lemon water to your laundry for a fresh, clean scent. A friend tells me it takes the stains out of linens.

Candy: Who doesn't like lemon drops?

Recipe for candied lemon slices: Bring 2 cups each sugar and water to a boil in a wide skillet. Add 2 thinly-sliced thin-skinned lemons; simmer 25 minutes, or until translucent. Cool in syrup. Remove, let syrup drip off. Use as a garnish.

Cleaning: I especially like lemon oil furniture polish.

Beauty: Wash hair with the juice of a lemon and then go out in the sunshine. This gives hair a luster.

Cooking: Wow! There are so many uses for our lemon in this category I am sure I can't begin to mention them all.

Flavor: Add lemon to a glass of water, hot tea, iced tea, squeeze over fish, lemon pepper chicken.

The other day I was reminiscing about my mother's Lemon Bisque Pie. I used to make my own graham cracker crust but now I buy the ready-made because they are so good. I was also thinking of a pudding my mother made, which was called Spanish Cream. This was a two-layered pudding. The bottom layer had the consistency of vanilla pudding and the top layer the consistency of Junket, and was lighter in color. Sadly I don't have the recipe for this. Does anyone out there have it? I would appreciate it. My friend continues to experiment with this to see if she can match my favorite pudding as a child.

I enjoy watching the Food Network and I was surprised to see a chef fill the cavity of a turkey with chunks of lemons and oranges. I feel it is all right to mention the orange here as I feel they are first cousins. Another chef suggested using the rind of an orange; just cut around the center of the orange. Place in a pan, cover with water and bring to a boil. Add your fresh green beans and cook. The rind gives the beans added flavor. Also try placing a lemon in the microwave for 10 seconds, which makes it juicier.

Frosting: Stir 2 tablespoons grated lemon zest and 1 1/2 tablespoons juice into a 16-oz. can of white frosting. Chill one hour.

Salad dressing: Whisk 3 tablespoons lemon juice, 1 tablespoon mustard and 1/4 teaspoon each of salt and pepper to blend. Slowly whisk in 1/2 cup oil; makes 3/4 of a cup.

Now I give you recipes using the lemon. I hope you have enjoyed my tribute to the lemon. I had fun coming up with the many, varied uses for this popular fruit.

Lemon Bisque Pie
During one of my mother's visits she made this dessert one night for dinner and it has been a favorite of my family ever since. Pies will be light and fluffy and guaranteed to melt in your mouth.
1 pkg. lemon Jello
1 1/4 c. boiling water
1/2 cup sugar
1 lemon (grated rind and juice)

Dissolve above ingredients into boiling water and let sit lightly. Prepare graham cracker crust with 1 1/2 c. crumbs, 1 stick (1/4 lb.) margarine or butter, and 3 tbsp. sugar. This makes two 8" pie crusts. Bake in 350 degree oven until crispness desired. Save some crumbs for top of pies.

Beat slightly-thickened Jello mixture.

Whip 1 can evaporated milk, which has been refrigerated for at least 24 hours. (Canned milk should be kept in refrigerator for safer storage, and then too, it is always well chilled for use. If milk has been stored too long before refrigeration, it will not whip.)

Gradually add Jello mixture, still whipping milk. Fill pie crusts and sprinkle remaining crumbs on top. Keep in refrigerator till ready to serve.

Easy Cake
1 pkg. Duncan Hines Lemon Cake Mix
1 pkg. instant lemon pudding
4 eggs
1/2 c. Crisco oil
1 c. water

Mix for five minutes in mixer and pour into lightly greased tube pan and bake in 350 degree pre-heated oven for 50 minutes.

Glazed icing:
1 c. confectioners sugar
2 tsp. lemon juice

Drizzle over cake while still warm. For a variation of this cake try a package of vanilla cake mix and vanilla pudding, chocolate cake mix and chocolate pudding or spice cake mix and butterscotch pudding. In your icing use vanilla flavoring instead of lemon juice.

Cranberry Spice Nut Bread
1/2 c. sugar
1 c. milk
1 egg, beaten
1/4 tsp. salt
1/4 tsp. ginger
1/2 st. cinnamon
1 tsp. lemon extract
3 c. biscuit mix
1 c. fresh cranberries, coarsely chopped
1/2 c. chopped walnuts

Preheat oven to 350 degrees. Combine sugar, milk and egg. Add salt, ginger, cinnamon, lemon extract and biscuit mix; beat vigorously for 30 seconds. Fold in cranberries and nuts. Spoon into well-greased 9" x 5" x 3" loaf pan. Bake for 60 to 65 minutes, or until loaf is browned. Remove from pan and cool thoroughly before slicing.

Cranberry Butter Jam
2 c. fresh cranberries
1 c. sugar
1/2 c. water
1/2 c. chopped walnuts
juice of 1 lemon
2 tbsp. butter or margarine

Combine cranberries, sugar and water in saucepan. Bring to a boil and cook, stirring occasionally, until cranberries begin to pop. Stir in walnuts, lemon juice and butter. Serve warm with above. Makes 2 1/2 cups.

March, 2007

Across the Table from

Linda Durrence

As we sat at Linda's dining room table over hot spiced tea we caught up on the happenings in our lives. I have known Linda and Gary Durrence since 1964, when they moved to Clayton in order for Gary to take a position with Burlington Industries in Rabun Gap. My husband Harry was also affiliated with Burlington, and the Durrences joined Clayton Baptist Church where we had our membership, so this added to the association with this family even more.

Linda was born in Clarkesville and Gary in south Georgia. They met in high school when Gary came to North Georgia Tech in Clarkesville on a basketball scholarship. Upon graduation Gary joined the Air Force and they lived in Bruswick, Georgia, Maine, and Kansas City, Missouri. After his tenure in the Air Force, Gary continued his education at Piedmont College and played basketball there, as well. They have two children - Chad, who works at Burger King and Kristen, who lives in Alpharetta. She is Director of Admissions for Mt. Pisgah Christian School.

When their children were growing up they called Linda a wonderful winter mother. They didn't see much of her in the summer because Linda went into real estate with Johnson & Johnson for 10 years. She was in customer service in Cornelia, a part of the Lumite Division of Johnson & Johnson. Then Linda joined

Century-21 Poss Realty. Gary is now retired from Burlington, where he was employed for 25 years.

Linda loves to cook and entertain and learned this early on from her mother. Linda's father had charge of the Royal Ambassadors of the Baptist church there in Clarkesville as well as helping with the basketball team, so there were always people coming and going through the home.

Linda's mother is now 89 years young. She spends some time with Linda and with her other daughter in Carrollton, as well as at the homeplace in Clarkesville. They are a very close-knit family and enjoy vacationing together at their place on Lake Burton. Gary and Linda also love to travel and take two or three nice trips a year.

As I said, Linda loves to cook. One time when the children were away she decided to put a turkey breast into the oven, in order for her and Gary to have turkey sandwiches and easy meals. She wrapped the turkey breast in aluminum foil and turned the oven on high, then turned the heat to very low. Since the children were away, Linda and Gary were out more and often went to a restaurant instead of preparing meals. One night when they came in Gary asked why the oven was on. This was two days after Linda had placed the turkey breast in the oven. There was dinner, burned to a crisp and about the size of a fist. It went into the garbage immediately. The family just loves to tease Linda about this. When asked how she cooks a turkey breast she just replies, "Turn the oven on low, bake for two days and throw it away."

The recipes Linda shares with us can be found in "The Rabun County Board of Realtors Cook Book." I have a copy and it is just wonderful; you will want one for yourself.

. I appreciate so much that Linda took time out of her busy schedule to be interviewed as I enjoyed our visit thoroughly.

You will note as you read the recipes they are all from the family, with the exception of the Refrigerated Rolls. The recipe was given to Linda by a friend and was used at the old Green Hotel on Main Street next to the Methodist church in Clayton.

So now enjoy using these recipes and thank you again, Linda, for affording me such a pleasant morning.

Broccoli Casserole
This is from Linda's sister and is a family favorite.

2 pkgs. frozen, chopped broccoli
1 c. sharp cheese, grated
1/2 c. onions, chopped
1/2 c. mayonnaise
1 stick butter, melted and divided
2 eggs
1/2 can cream of mushroom soup
1/2 c. cheese Ritz cracker crumbs

Cook broccoli according to directions. Omit the salt. Drain thoroughly. Add cheese, onions, mayonnaise, half the butter, eggs and mushroom soup in baking dish. Set aside. Mix remaining butter and cracker crumbs. Spread on top of casserole. Bake at 350 degrees for approximately 30 minutes

Refrigerator Rolls

1 c. shortening
1/2 c. sugar
1 1/2 tsp. salt
1 c. boiling water

Pour boiling water over other ingredients, blend well and cool.

2 pkgs. dry yeast
1 c. warm water

Dissolve yeast in warm water. Mix 2 eggs, beaten with all the above ingredients. Then sift and measure 6 cups plain flour. Add to the above. Cover and let stand in refrigerator several hours. When ready to use, form into balls, let double in size and bake at 415 degrees until brown. Dough may be kept in refrigerator several days. These are wonderful rolls and always a big hit.

Best Punch Recipe in the World

5 c. water
5 c. sugar
2 (3 oz.) pkgs. Jello (I use orange.)
2 sm. cans frozen orange juice, add water according to directions
2 lg. cans pineapple juice
4 sm. cans frozen lemonade, add water according to directions

Put water and sugar and Jello in a pot and heat to boiling. Mix with fruit juices. Put in gallon plastic milk jugs to 3/4 full. Put in freezer and shake every 2 hours.

Linda's Red Velvet Cake

2 1/2 c. all-purpose flour
1 tsp. soda
1 tsp. salt
1 1/2 c. sugar
1 c. buttermilk
1 3/4 c. vegetable oil
2 eggs
1 tsp. vanilla
2 oz. red food coloring
1 tsp. vinegar

Frosting

1 (8 oz.) pkg. cream cheese, softened
1/2 c. butter, softened
1 box 4X powdered sugar
1 tsp. vanilla

Sift dry ingredients together. Cream sugar, milk, eggs, and oil. Blend dry ingredients into creamed mixture. Add vanilla, coloring, and vinegar. Turn into 3 greased and floured 8-inch layer pans. Bake in preheated 350-degree oven for 30 minutes. Cool, then frost.

Frosting directions: Mix all ingredients except vanilla in the mixer until smooth. Add vanilla and mix well. Spread on cooled cake. I sprinkle each layer with finely-chopped pecans and then cover the top and sides of the cake with large pieces of pecans.

This recipe is another family favorite. One of Linda's nephews requested it for the "groom's cake" at his wedding.

April, 2007

Across the Table from

Ginny Bryan

Today I am interviewing Ginny Bryan who holds the position of Administrative Assistant focusing in Administration & Children's Ministries here at Clayton Baptist Church. She has been with us for almost nine years now, coming here in 1998. Ginny is most efficient in her position and is so much more to us than this. She is very caring and is always tuned to the needs of others. I know of her love and support firsthand as she ministered to my husband when he died. Another time, she heard I needed help, drove into my driveway and took me to the emergency room, which was where I needed to be at the time. We are so blessed here at Clayton Baptist Church in having Ginny as part of our staff.

Ginny grew up in metro Atlanta and was the third of four children. Her mother was a stay-at-home mom tending to her son and three daughters.

Prior to coming to the Clayton Baptist Church she was administrator of a personal care home; then went into church work, similar to the position she now holds. She was also a loan officer and bank branch manager. It was during this time that she met Randy, her husband. He used to ride with his partner in the police force to the bank where Ginny worked, as his friend was on the Board of Directors of the bank. Ginny and Randy started dating and were married eight months later. Ginny's usual Saturday lunch was hot dogs and grilled cheese sandwiches and when Randy first tasted this he thought Ginny was a gourmet cook. He had lived alone for a while and was used to frozen meals.

The Bryans are a blended family, as Randy brought two daughters into the marriage and Ginny, one daughter. Together they have a son, Buck, who is now attending Georgia Tech. - GO JACKETS. They adopted another son, Charlie, when he was 22 months old. She adds that he is single and looking. He works here in Clayton with Clayton Family Activities Therapy as encourager. He also sings in the Sanctuary Choir.

The Bryans enjoy entertaining in their home that Ginny designed herself, one that would meet their individual needs, so she is talented in many areas. Their most treasured guests are family, 18 to 28 people on Thanksgiving and Easter; and having Easter egg hunts. Thanksgiving begins the preparations for the coming Christmas holiday and Ginny's use of Christmas China and decorations is begun. They not only celebrate birthdays, but celebrate birthday week, when the honoree chooses the menu and cake of choice.

On one such occasion Ginny baked her much requested Red Velvet Cake and the whole three pans actually bubbled in the oven and exploded like a volcano. There was no time to make another and the outside rim of the cakes tasted very good. Ginny tried in vain to salvage her prize cake, but nothing worked. She found that she had mistakenly used self-rising flour. So she used her intuition and decided to make a Trifle instead. It looked beautiful and everyone praised it. Ginny told them it was the newest rage here in the mountains, that of a Red Velvet Trifle. She confessed her mistake later in the day, but the family still requests this at gatherings. I recently baked a cake for a youth function at the church and made a mistake in the recipe. I was ready to throw it out but remembered Ginny's Trifle, salvaged it and I do believe it was the best

Swiss Chardinaire

1/4 cup olive oil
1 small zucchini squash halved and sliced
1 small yellow squash halved and sliced
3-5 garlic cloves minced
1 bunch swiss chard sliced widthwise
1/4 cup pine nuts
feta cheese

Saute squash, garlic for about 5 minutes, the add Swiss chard and turn over several times until wilted. Add pine nuts, top with crumbled Feta cheese. Serve over brown rice or plain as a side vegetable

Okra Facile

1/4 cup olive oil
1/2 to 3/4 lb. okra (small pods)
  (remove heads)
1/2 tbsp. kosher salt (optional)

Saute okra in olive oil for about 5 minutes or until tender

Easy Collard Greens

1/4 cup olive oil
1 small onion halved and sliced
1 bunch fresh collards sliced widthwise

Saute onions in olive oil until tender. Add collard greens and turn several times until wilted about 5 minutes.

Easy Refrigerator Cake

1 pint heavy whipping cream
Hershey's chocolate
2 round yellow cake layers sliced widthwise
make 4 round layers

Whip cream and add chocolate syrup until mocha colored and ice all 4 layers, stacking one on top of the other and then ice the outside (this is an old family recipe that is so easy and delicious)

Oriental Cole Slaw

1 bag of tricolor Slaw (cabbage, carrot,
  purple cabbage)
1 bag of chicken flavored Ramen noodles
1/4 cup of sunflower seeds
1/4 cup sliced almonds
4-6 sliced scallions
oil and vinegar to taste

Lightly roast sunflower seeds and almond slices in toaster oven. Put slaw in a bowl.
Add Ramen noodles after they have been broken up on hard surface (do not cook noodles--reluctantly add them dry) Add packet of flavoring. Add oil and vinegar and nuts and seeds. Add scallions. Toss and refrigerate for 12 hours. Salt and pepper to taste (I use a little Soy Sauce)

June, 2007

Across the Table from

Patsy & Chuck Rosenberry

I love writing for the Laurel. It finds me reuniting with friends I have known down through the years, and also affords me the opportunity to meet new friends. Such is the case this month, when I introduced myself to Patsy and Chuck Rosenberry in Bell Colony.

Patsy met me at the door and we stepped out to the deck off their living-dining room. Wow! What a fantastic view, and I can imagine the many pleasant hours they spend here relaxing.

There is a third member of this family, a tri-colored Lhasa Apso named Chelsea. She is number trained, as Chuck once had an attack dog trained this way, but there is a vast difference between the two dogs. Chelsea knows the meaning of the numbers given for command, but pretty much ignores them and does as she pleases. She is such a cute dog--who wouldn't let her have her way?

Patsy was born and raised in Atlanta in the Avondale area, and had one son and one daughter. She later moved to Hattiesburg, Mississippi and was in the medical field for 40 years. She was a single mom at that time, and also worked three nights a week in a restaurant.

Chuck was brought up in Wyoming where his father was a rancher. He loved the outdoor life and enjoyed hunting. His father was recognized as the World Champion saddle breakers rider, who then went into construction after World War II. They moved about, and Chuck lived in Wyoming, Phoenix, Denver, and Idaho, and this was all while he was in the first grade.

He joined the Air Force, and then went with General Electric in Washington and was associated with the Manhattan Project. He also lived in Las Vegas and Hattiesburg, and he held the position of head of clean up after tests were completed. His job was to examine the deer and fish, looking for updates to the food chain of the native animals after testing was complete. He looked at the lungs and kidneys. This was at the Nevada Test site known as The Tatum Dome Test Site.

While in Hattiesburg, he and his buddies frequented a restaurant there and he met this lovely waitperson whose name was Patsy. They met in June and married the next April. Chuck adopted the two children, who were 10 and 12 years old at that time. Now they have two granddaughters who live in Las Vegas and Salt Lake City, respectively.

While in Las Vegas, they took part in many commercials and along the way they met Dick Wilson and his wife Meg. How many of you remember Mr. Whipple, who asked us please not to squeeze the Charmin? He was one and the same. He was such a lovable, gentle man that to this day, my household still chooses Charmin.

On one of their vacations, Patsy and Chuck visited her sister who lives here on Charlie Mountain, and wanted to take them around the county to see the many sights. They chose to sit on the deck and take in the view, falling in love with the area. Patsy asked her sister to look around for a house for them. Once you have the opportunity to be in Rabun County, who can resist wanting to live here? Her sister found a house in Bell Colony. They looked at the house with the fantastic view in February and moved here in April.

The three of us enjoyed the Easy Fried Pies with our coffee. One could not tell they were not made from scratch. Patsy is known for her wonderful meals, which she enjoys preparing in her kitchen. It has corner windows allowing her to bring the outside in while cooking. One end of the kitchen opens to another deck where Chuck grills and smokes many meals.

Patsy gives us her recipe for her Very Special Lasagne, along with the Easy Fried Pies we enjoyed together. There are some folks you meet for the first time, who make you feel comfortable from the beginning, and the Rosenberrys are such a couple.

A Very Special Lasagne
And it really is. It is rich and so delicate in texture and flavors that it becomes an elegant dish for a first course or entree.

1/2 pound lasagne noodles
1 pound ground beef
1/2 cup chopped onion
3 cloves garlic, minced
1 tablespoon olive oil
3 pounds tomatoes (6-7 large), peeled, seeded, chopped (or canned tomatoes, drained)
1 1/2 teaspoons seasoned salt
2 tablespoons chopped parsley (or 1 tsp. dried)
1 teaspoon basil (if you are fortunate enough to have fresh basil, use 2 tablespoons chopped)
1/2 teaspoon oregano
1/4 teaspoon freshly ground pepper

Cook lasagne noodles in boiling, salted water until "al dente," still firm to the bite. Drain and keep them in cold water until ready to use.

Saute ground beef, onion, and garlic in olive oil until meat is no longer pink. Add remaining ingredients and cook at a fast simmer until sauce is quite thick (about 30-40 minutes). Skim fat. Preheat oven to 400.

Bechamel
1/2 cup butter
4 tablespoons flour
1 cup milk
1 cup chicken broth
1 chicken bouillon cube (optional)
1/8 teaspoon salt

Melt butter, add flour and cook, stirring with a whisk, for one minute. Slowly add milk and chicken broth and bring to a boil, still using whisk. Taste and add chicken bouillon cube, if needed. Add salt.

Ricotta Filling
1 egg
1/2 pound ricotta cheese
1/4 cup grated Parmesan cheese
1/16-1/8 teaspoon nutmeg
1/2 teaspoon salt

Beat egg in a bowl. Add remaining ingredients and stir well with a fork

Cheeses
1 1/2 cups grated Parmesan cheese
4 ounces mozzarella cheese, sliced
4 ounces teleme cheese
Butter

In the following order, layer in a lightly-greased 13 x 9-inch baking dish: a little meat sauce, half of the noodles, half of the remaining meat sauce, 1/2 cup Bechamel, 1/2 cup Parmesan cheese, half of the mozzarella, teleme, and ricotte; the remaining noodles and meat sauce, 1/2 cup Bechamel, 1/2 cup Parmesan cheese. Dot with butter. At this point, the dish may be covered and refrigerated. From room temperature, bake at 400 degrees, uncovered, for 30 minutes for more, until bubbly.

This dish freezes well.

Easy Fried Pies
1 pkg. dried fruit (apples or peaches)
1/4 to 1/2 cup sugar (according to taste)
1/2 teaspoon cinnamon
pinch of nutmeg
8-10 flour tortillas (small)

Cook fruit until tender, add sugar and spices. Add tablespoon of cooked and seasoned fruit to tortilla and fry in 1 inch of hot oil, until brown. Flip and brown the other side.

Fast and Easy!!

July, 2007

Across the Table from

Janis & Coleman Jones

As I pulled into their driveway, a most delightful aroma coming from the house greeted me. As soon as I stepped inside, I was made to feel welcome by Janis and Coleman Jones. We sat down at their dining room table and had refreshments which consisted of Janis' Shrimp Dip and crackers, along with our beverage.

It was so enjoyable getting to know this couple as we sat watching the cardinals and squirrels through a large window in this room which includes a made-to-order cook's delight kitchen. It is large and airy and needs to be, since they cook together every night. They have been doing this since they started dating.

When they check in with one another during the day, they do not discuss what restaurant they will visit that night or who will bring home take-out food. They discuss their menu for the night. This is a special time for the two of them as they prepare dinner together.

Coleman also enjoys cooking on the grill three or four times a week. They showed me their outdoor patio where they enjoy entertaining and where they also grow their own herbs. After dinner, they watch a movie together. Janis and Coleman are such a lovely couple and I can imagine they havemucg fun deciding just what movie suits their mood for the evening.

Janis is native Californian where she was a legal secretary for a large corporation. Upon moving here, she managed The Old Edwards Inn and another in the Highlands area. She then decided to change careers and went back to school to become a nail technician in order to open her own shop known as "Expectations" in Mountain City.

Coleman was also raised in California and became acquainted with Rabun County when his parents moved here. He has been with Duvall Ford Company for three years in the company's Chevrolet division. He moved to Rabun County in 1996.

This couple met in California in a small town in the southern part of the state near Sierra Madre, which begins in the foothills of the San Gabriel Mountains. Their family consists of three children who are all grown, since the couple has been married for 25 years.

Their eldest son lives in California; their middle daughter lives in Dallas, Texas with their granddaughter who is three years old. Their youngest son lived in Colorado, but since his position requires much traveling, he had made his headquarters here in Rabun County.

Janis and Coleman belong to the Rabun Gap Presbyterian Church where Coleman was chosen as an Elder. They also have property on Lake Hartwell to enjoy as a get-away.

We then enjoyed Janis' Lasagna Soup with Spiced Parmesan bread sticks. The soup is absolutely delicious and tastes like lasagna. I was supplied with enough to take home to enjoy yet another time. This thoughtful couple was also taking dinner to her parents, as this was moving day for them.

After our nice visit, Coleman helped by backing my car out of their driveway, thus pointing me in the right direction to head home. As I looked out my rearview mirror, I saw this couple walking toward their house, holding hands – a perfect ending to a perfect day.

Janis and Coleman, thank you for such a delightful visit. Continue to enjoy each other and the labor of the love of cooking you share each evening.

Braised Country Ribs

2 lbs. Country style pork ribs
1 large yellow onion
Killer Barbecue Sauce (next recipe)
1 tablespoon olive oil
1 28 oz. can diced tomatoes
1 14.5 oz. can beef broth
Kosher salt
Chili powder
Garlic powder

Heat olive oil in a Dutch oven. Pre-heat oven to 300 degrees F. Season pork ribs with salt, garlic, and chili powder. Slice onion in rings. Brown up ribs in batches, and set aside. Sear the meat well. Add onions to the same pot and cook for about 5 minutes, stirring to deglaze. Drain about half the liquid from the diced tomatoes. Combine one or even two batches of Killer Barbecue Sauce, diced tomatoes, and ¾ can of beef broth in a bowl and whisk it up. Put a layer of ribs in the pot on top of the onion. Add just enough of the Barbecue sauce/tomato mixture to cover, then add the next layer of ribs. Cover that with the remaining sauce mixture. Ribs should be covered with liquid. Layer the ribs "tic-tac-toe." Cover the Dutch oven with a layer of foil and then put the top on. Braise at 300 degrees F for 30 minutes. Reduce heat to 250 degrees F and braise for another hour, up to an hour and a half, maximum. Serve with rice, rice and beans, sweet potatoes, corn on the cob… you know what to do!!

Killer Barbecue Sauce
(This is Coleman's own recipe)

12 oz. Bottle Heinz chili sauce
8 oz. Maple syrup
2 tablespoons Dijon mustard
3 shakes liquid smoke
4 shakes Worcestershire sauce
8 – 10 shakes tobasco
1 ½ teaspoons chili powder
1 tablespoon dark brown sugar
1 tablespoon dark molasses
Up to ¼ cup cider vinegar
2 good pinches dried oregano
3 garlic cloves minced
2 good pinches dried basil

Combine all ingredients in a quart Mason jar and shake it up well. Pour into a saucepan and heat slowly until just about a boil. Don't cook it.

Lasagna Soup

1 lb. ground Italian sausage
2 cups onions, chopped
1 cup carrot, diced
2 cups button mushrooms, sliced
2 tablespoons garlic, minced
4 cups chicken broth
1 can diced Italian-style-stewed tomatoes (14 ½)
1 cup mafalda pasta, see below
2 cups fresh spinach, chopped
1 cup provolone or fresh mozzarella, diced
¼ cup parmesan, shredded
4 teaspoons thinly sliced fresh basil
* Mini lasagna; or campenelle; cook pasta in soup!

Brown sausage in a large saucepan over medium-high heat. Add onion and carrot; sauté 3 minutes. Strir in mushrooms and garlic, and sauté another 3 minutes. Add broth and tomatoes; bring to a boil. Stir in the pasta and simmer until cooked, about 10 minutes (or according to package directions). Add the spinach and cook about 1 minute, or until wilted.

To serve: place cubes of cheese in each serving bowl, then ladle soup over to melt. Garnish with Parmesan and basil. Serves 4.

August, 2007

Across the Table from

Shannon & Jack Alley

A thunderstorm was brewing as Shannon Alley and I sat in her lovely kitchen-dining area in her home in Tiger. We chatted and got to know one another better, and the storm just faded into the background in our cozy setting.

Shannon was born and raised here in Rabun County, the daughter of Nora Taylor Garland and Raleigh Garland. Her parents owned Garland's Grocery Store on old 441 north, that is now the Habitat for Humanity building, and the Garland home sat next door. Shannon is the middle of seven and has three brothers and three sisters. She had a lot of fun growing up with them and playing with her Taylor cousins.

The Garlands attended the North Clayton Baptist Church which her mother began as a Sunday School class in their living room. J.F. Marchman headed up the Rabun County Baptist Association and taught the class. As the congregation grew, they set up a tent and added Bible School which was the start of the church.

I remember shopping at Garland's Grocery Store and my mother always enjoyed her visits with them. Mrs. Garland gave me her recipe for Fruit Cocktail Cake that I included in my column written for the local newspaper in 1964. Shannon tells me that many folks prepare this in a sheet cake now, but I always thought it presented so nicely as a layered cake.

Jack was born and raised here in Wiley. Many of you remember Alley's Grocery Store. This belonged to his uncle. Jack graduated from Lakemont High School and went away to the army and served in Korea.

Later, they would meet at dances held in the high school gym here in Clayton and one night he asked if he could take her home. She agreed. They were married when Shannon was 19 years old. They lived in Atlanta for a while where Jack was with General Motors.

When they were first married and money was short (we can all relate to this), Jack insisted on cooking the meat as he did not want to take a chance on its not turning out right. Jack also enjoyed cooking along with Shannon, and when she didn't know what to have for dinner, he always suggested that she make a pone of corn bread or a pan of biscuits and the rest would take care of itself. Shannon found this to be true.

They decided they wanted to return to Rabun County. This is no surprise to many of us who did the same thing; I know we did. Shannon and Jack have five children, three girls and two boys, 10 grandchildren and three great-grandchildren.

When I first stepped into Shannon's home, she offered me a cup of coffee and a piece of pound cake. Since I'd just eaten lunch, I had to decline, but said that I would take a piece home with me. It smelled delicious and was still warm from the oven. In fact, Shannon gave me two pieces – one for me and one for a friend I was planning to dabble in acrylics with later that afternoon. I must confess, I kept both pieces. Shannon takes this cake to fundraisers and it has brought as much as $100.00 – no wonder – it was so good!

I found that Shannon also paints in acrylics and she showed me a picture of a flower she did, which was excellent. This is a very talented lady, who also once wrote a column for the local newspaper which I always enjoyed. She gave me a copy of a poem she wrote to her mother, which is very touching.

I so enjoyed my visit with you, Shannon. As I said, this is a very talented lady and do hope she gets back into her writing in the near future.

Broccoli-Cauliflower Salad

1 bunch broccoli finely chopped
1 head cauliflower finely chopped
1 ½ cups grated carrots
1 large tomato finely chopped
Dressing
1 cup mayonnaise
2 teaspoons prepared mustard
2 teaspoons vinegar
Dash of Worcestershire sauce
Salt and pepper to taste

Make dressing and pour over vegetables. Mix well and chill thoroughly. Serves 10-12. It is a great salad for a cook-out for a covered-dish affair.

Brunswick Stew
Quick, easy and delicious!

2 pounds ground beef
3 onions chopped
2 cans creamed corn
1 bottle (24 oz.) ketchup
4 o r 5 medium potatoes
½ cup white vinegar
4 chicken breasts
2 quarts tomato juice
2 cans whole kernel corn
¼ cup Worcestershire sauce
1 stick butter
1 tablespoon brown sugar

Brown and cook beef with onions until done. Boil the chicken, and then chop. Cook chopped potatoes separately.

In a large pot or crock pot, mix tomato juice, ketchup, salt, pepper and hot sauce to taste. Add the meat and other ingredients, except potatoes, and vinegar. Bring to a boil and cook for 20 minutes. Add potatoes and simmer for 30 minutes. Add vinegar and stir.

Salmon Steaks Teriyaki

4 salmon steaks, approximately ½ inch thick
½ tsp. sesame oil
4 tsp. soy sauce
2 tsp. Lemon juice
1 garlic clove, minced
1 tbsp. butter, melted

Place steaks in a shallow pan. Mix remaining ingredients except butter and pour over salmon. Let stand 20 minutes at room temperature, turning occasionally. Remove steaks from marinade and brush both sides with melted butter. Broil 5 to 7 minutes on each side until browned and easily flaked. Serves 4.

Mrs. R.L. Garland's Fruit Cocktail Cake

2 cups plain flour
2 cups sugar
2 eggs
1 tsp. Soda
½ tsp. Salt
1 303 can fruit cocktail
Topping (recipe below)

Mix all cake ingredients except topping and stir by hand until well-mixed. Bake at 300 degrees for 45 minutes.

Topping
½ cup canned milk
1 cup coconut
1 cup sugar
1 stick margarine

Cook over low heat for 10 minutes and spread over cooled layers. Enjoy!

Hint: I baked this recipe in two layers and it was so high and pretty. I was really proud of myself, but the credit goes to Mrs. Garland for her delicious recipe.

September, 2007

Across the Table from

Karla Sidey
& Family

As Karla and I sat in the MAC of the Clayton Baptist Church, we looked at the pictures of the youth of the church enjoying their Super Bowl Party which was held at Karla's house. They enjoyed playing pool, games, eating and just having a good time being together. Karla is quite a remarkable lady as you will see as you read on.

Karla Sidey bought property here about six years ago, and moved here three years later when the house in Heatherstone was completed. Her husband was killed in a car accident ten years ago by a teen-ager who was driving under the influence. Karla was expecting her daughter, Lindsey, at the time and she delivered seven weeks later.

They are members of the Clayton Baptist Church and are quite active in the youth of our church; she also helps in the nursery. The children are all doing well in school and the three oldest boys have participated in Mission trips here and in Florida. Karla had just dropped off Christopher and Douglas at band practice and Douglas made Lions Club All-State Band.

Karla's father was in the printing business and they moved all over the country. Her mother was a Home Economics major and was a stay at home mom. Karla loves to cook and she was fortunate enough to have wonderful help along the way. Her dad still makes biscuits like no one else and her children gather around him in the kitchen when he is visiting to ask if they may help him.

Her mother-in-law also played an important part in teaching her how to cook. This talent has carried over to her children as they enjoy gathering in the kitchen to cook with their mother. Her son always talks about the wonderful birthday cakes Karla has made down through the years. Their favorite things to prepare are sushi, pasta and ice cream. Her grandmother is 94 years young and still makes everything from scratch.

While in Florida, after her husband was killed, Karla joined a support group entitled, "Hearts and Hope." They met weekly and had potluck dinners and also had age appropriate groups for the children. She received much support and made many friends through these meetings.

When Karla was 16 years old, a friend encouraged her to enter a pie-baking contest. Karla prepared her Woven Raisin Pie that she shares with us today--and she won. Later on she also had a dessert business of her own in Florida. I told you she is quite a remarkable lady, but wait. I noted the cutest purse she was carrying that day. It was made of old jeans and trimmed in colorful patterns and was also reversible.

Karla has a business named Karla's Kreations. All advertising is by word of mouth at this point. I would like to add that one of these purses would make a wonderful gift for that special friend or even yourself. I would love to have one and you may call 706-746-0091.

I would like to introduce the children more. Benjamin is 19, Christopher is 15, Douglas is 14, Nathan is 11 and Lindsey turns 10 this month, and then there is Juli who is 7.

Oh, did I mention that Karla just painted a mural on her daughter's bedroom wall? Is there no end to this lady's talents? WOW.

Needless to say, I was most impressed with Karla's accomplishments and the way in which she has taken hold of her life after her tragic experience. It was good meeting you and thank you for the time you took from your busy schedule to be interviewed. Thank you again!

Woven Raisin Pie

1 c. brown sugar
2 Tbsp. cornstarch
2 c. raisins
1/2 teaspoon grated orange rind
2 Tbsp. lemon juice
1 1/3 c. water
1/2 c. chopped walnuts
Pastry for a double crust
1 Tbsp milk
1 Tbsp. sugar

Combine brown sugar and cornstarch in a saucepan. Stir in raisins, orange rind, orange juice, lemon rind, lemon juice, and water. Cook and stir over medium heat until thickened. Remove from heat and sir in walnuts. Cool slightly while rolling out pie crust. Line a pie plate with pastry. Fill with mixture. Roll out second pastry. Cut pastry in 1/2 " strips. Place the longest strip across center of filling. Place the next longest strip in the opposite direction. Continue this pattern, weaving them together to form a lattice crust. Pinch and flute edges together. Brush lattice crust with milk and sprinkle with sugar. Bake at 375° for 35-40 minutes.

Lime Scallops

5 Tbsp. butter, divided
2 teaspoons grated lime rind
1 teaspoon ground ginger
1 Tbsp, olive oil
2 pounds sea scallops
4 Tbsp. lime juice
1/2 c. walnut pieces
Fresh parsley for garnish

In mini Cuisinart, puree 4 Tbsp. butter, lime rind, and ginger together. Remove from bowl and shape into log. Wrap in plastic and place in freezer.

Heat oil and 1 T. butter in large sauté pan over high heat. Pat scallops dry. Add the scallops and heat until golden, stirring occasionally. Pour off the fat. Stir in the lime juice and cook 1 minute. Turn the heat down to low. Remove lime butter from freezer. Cut into slices. Add 1 slice at a time to the sauté pan. Cook until it makes a thick sauce. Stir in walnuts. Garnish with parsley and serve immediately.

Pasta with our favorite sauces,
Clam Sauce and Pesto

Cooked and drained pasta

Clam Sauce

4 (8 oz) cans of minced clams
1/4 c. olive oil
4 cloves garlic, pressed
1/4 c. fresh parsley, chopped
1/4 c. white wine
12 fresh basil leaves, chopped
1/2 teaspoon salt

Drain clams, reserving clam juice. Cook garlic in hot olive oil. Stir in clam juice and remaining ingredients, except clams. Cook about 10-12 minutes, stirring occasionally. Stir in clams. Cook just until clams are heated through. Serve immediately over hot pasta.

Pesto

1 c. olive oil
1 c. Romano cheese
1/4 c. fresh parsley, chopped
6 cloves garlic
1 c. packed fresh basil leaves
1 teaspoon salt

Place all ingredients in a blender and puree until smooth. Serve immediately over pasta.

October, 2007

Across the Table from

Carol Brown & Lisa Free

Lisa Free (left) and Carol Brown (right)

While enjoying lunch at The Old Clayton Inn, I had a conversation with my waitress, Carol Brown, about the joy of ladies deer hunting. Carol and I talked about recipes for venison and how good deer meat is for you. Carol was sharing with me that there is a danger of the ladies only hunt being stopped due to lack of participation. This year instead of a four-day hunt, it has been cut back to three days. I suggested that, to raise awareness of the hunt it might be fun to share some of her recipes for preparing venison.

My good friend Jean Emhart is taking this issue off, so I will try to do as well with Rabun's Recipes as she does. I met with Carol Brown and her hunting companion, Lisa Free, at The Old Clayton Inn to find out what drives them to make this ladies-only hunt a priority. Both Carol and Lisa agreed they enjoy hunting, but more so, they enjoy the time away from it all. More and more women are stressed from working full time, keeping a home and raising a family, and have very little, if any, "me time".

A hunt often begins before the sun comes up. A hunter makes her way through the woods to the tree stand or ground blind before nature wakes up. Carol spoke of watching the earth come to life. The sun rises, the birds start their morning melodies and the squirrels busy themselves gathering acorns. The smell of the woods during deer season is magnificent, and as you sit there amazed by all God has created, lost in the silence, a leaf falls slowly to the forest floor.

Being this close with nature is beneficial to the soul and mind of any hunter, but women whose lives are so full are rejuvenated by this time alone. Many times, the elusive whitetail is not even seen during a hunt, but Lisa and Carol each told me that hunting is about so much more than harvesting a deer. Although the experience of taking a deer is one that both ladies have enjoyed, it is not the number one priority. What is it that these two women enjoy about hunting together? The camaraderie, camping, cooking, sitting around the campfire talking and laughing with absolutely no distractions, it is the "me time"

Ladies of all ages take advantage of the opportunity to hunt. Carol had never hunted when Lisa invited her to join her, and they hunted together. They laughed about being in the woods for four days without a bath, Carol said you learn pretty fast that bathing in the creek is not that bad. Both ladies agreed that they are honored by the privilege to have a hunt that is just for the ladies.

The Georgia Department of Natural Resources offers other special hunts besides the ladies-only hunts. There are dates set aside for Parent-Child hunts, and a Wheelchair hunt for disabled hunters, and then there is the Georgia Hunters for the Hungry program which allows hunters to help fight hunger by donating the meat from their harvest to feed the hungry. Since 1993 Georgia hunters have donated nearly 200,000 pounds of venison, and that is awesome.

The uses for venison are numerous. Carol, Lisa and I agreed that you can substitute ground venison for any recipe that calls for ground beef: soup, spaghetti, chili, meatloaf, and more. A deer roast can be cooked with potatoes, carrots, and onions, or stewed and pulled apart, smothered in your favorite barbecue sauce and served on a bun.

Anyone who has ever eaten deer tenderloin knows it is the cream of the crop, whether you slice it thin and roll it in flour and seasonings and fry it, or if you leave it whole, rub it with your favorite seasonings and wrap it in bacon and cook it in the oven or on the grill. It is by far the finest!

Lisa and Carol shared with me some new ways to prepare this lean and healthy meat. Thank you, Lisa and Carol for meeting with me, and for sharing their passion for hunting.

by Tracy McCoy

Carol Brown's Recipes:

BBQ Deer Roast

1 deer ham
10 red potatoes
8 carrots
3 onions
salt
pepper
garlic salt

Bake ham at 350 degrees for 1 ½ - 2 hours then add potatoes, carrots, and onion to roast. Add salt, pepper, and garlic salt and continue cooking for another hour or so until meat falls off the bone. When done, take vegetables out and pull the meat off the bone and add barbeque sauce to meat and stir it up. Serve with vegetables on the side. (This recipe can also be cooked without vegetables and meat can be served on a bun).

Deer Tips over Rice (Easy)

1 deer ham
pack of mushrooms
2 packs of beef gravy mix
salt and pepper
2 bags of Minute Rice

Cut meat off the bone in small chunks. Cook in crock pot with mushrooms and water all day until tender, drain all but 3 cups of water and then add 2 packs of gravy mix, salt and pepper, and cook till thickened. In a sauce pan boil 2 bags of Minute Rice. Drain water add salt to taste.

Serve deer tips and gravy over rice. Delicious!

Lisa Free's Recipes:

When having your deer prepared, ask your butcher to leave an extra portion of the loin attached to the ribs for these recipes.

Spicy Chinese Venison Ribs

4 or 5 lbs of venison ribs, cut apart
2/3 cup Kikkoman Sauce or Hoisin Sauce (comes in sweet and spicy, teriyaki or sweet and sour)
1 - 6 oz. can of tomato paste
1/3 cup sugar
1/4 cup rice vinegar
3 teaspoons of minced garlic
1 teaspoon hot pepper sauce

Preheat oven to 375 degrees
Arrange ribs in a single layer on a large baking sheet and set aside.

Mix remaining ingredients in a bowl, making a sauce. Pour mixture over ribs, turning ribs to coat them well. Cover ribs with aluminum foil and bake 30-45 minutes. Remove foil and bake uncovered for an additional 30 minutes or until liquid begins to thicken and meat is tender. Baste ribs occasionally by turning over.

Barbecued Venison Ribs

4-5 lbs of venison ribs cut apart
Sauce
2 tablespoons olive oil
1 medium onion
1 teaspoon of minced garlic
1 cup of honey
1 - 6 oz. can tomato paste
1 - 6 oz. can pineapple juice
2 tablespoons hot pepper sauce
2 tablespoons molasses
1 teaspoon ground cumin
1 teaspoon salt
1 teaspoon black pepper

Preheat oven to 375 degrees. Arrange ribs in a single layer on a large baking sheet.

In a saucepan, heat olive oil over medium heat, add onion and minced garlic and sauté stirring occasionally. Whisk in all of the remaining ingredients, and bring to boil. Reduce heat and simmer until sauce is slightly thickened, stirring often.

Pour sauce over ribs turning to coat. Cover with aluminum foil and bake for 30 minutes. Remove foil. Turn and coat ribs and bake uncovered for another 30 minutes or until liquid is thick and meat is tender.

INDEX OF RECIPES

BREADS
"The Rolls - literally"

DESSERTS
"The Sweet Treats"

DRINKS
"To wash it down"

THE SAUCES
"To Top it Of"

VINTAGE RABUN
A collection of Mountain History from M.E. Law
Due to release Spring 08

The Storyteller
A collection from the life of Janie P. Taylor
Due to release Summer 08

From the Hills
A COLLECTION OF ARTIST FROM THE GEORGIA MOUNTAIN LAUREL
Due to release Fall 08

Adventure Out
With Peter McIntosh

Your Guide to the Trails of the Mountains
Due to release Spring 09